PRAISE FOR RUNAWAY RADICAL

I devoured *Runaway Ra_____* _____ ____ony
that could save the next _____ _____ sary
hurt. This mother-and-s_____ _____ ant
mirror: in it, we see gra_____ ___ denial and the
profound pain when denial is stripped away.

—Brad Jersak, Senior Editor of *CWR Magazine*, Professor at
Westminster Theological Centre, Author of *A More Christlike God*

Runaway Radical is a captivating and embodied warning of what happens
when shame-based discipleship twists the mission of God. Yet it is also a
beautiful story of God's limitless grace and redemption that demonstrates the
center of all that we believe—that God is love. An important and timely book.

—Jamie Arpin-Ricci, Pastoral Leader at Little Flowers
Community, Codirector of YWAM Urban Ministries,
Winnipeg, Author of *Vulnerable Faith*

In *Runaway Radical,* I see a pattern I've found often throughout many years
of teaching young adults. Youth and idealism go together like cotton candy
at a carnival. And too much idealism—like too much cotton candy—usually
ends in a sickening downward crash. But *Runaway Radical* offers more than
a mere cautionary tale: Jonathan's story provides a helpful, healing, and hopeful corrective as he surrenders his radical idealism and exchanges it for the
full embrace of grace. This is a book I will recommend again and again to the
young, passionate idealists I am privileged to teach.

—Karen Swallow Prior, PhD, Author of *Booked: Literature
in the Soul of Me* and *Fierce Convictions: The Extraordinary
Life of Hannah More—Poet, Reformer, Abolitionist*

Runaway Radical is, in its purest form, a story of radical love. It is Jonathan
Hollingsworth's radical love of God and his fellow man which propels the nar-
rative and his journey to Africa. It is Amy Hollingsworth's radical love for her
son which propels her to support his effort while likely foreseeing the inevitable fall through the thin ice of idealism. It is their radical love for each other
and their shared Heavenly Father that gives them the courage to share this
cautionary tale of melding the perfection of God's call with the imperfection
of God's people. Finally, it is my radical love for the count-it-all-loss-but-for-
Christ risk takers that kept me turning the pages and wanting Jonathan to win
in the end. And the "win"? The knowledge that when the eyes of God run to
and fro across the earth he finds one who said "yes." Well done, son. Well done.

—Kathy Chiero, Host of *The Sitting Room* Radio Program

What happens when you give God everything, and he doesn't live up to his end of the bargain? In this page-turning story, Amy and Jonathan show that it's not about how radical we are but how great his grace is.

—JOSH KELLEY, SPEAKER, AUTHOR OF *RADICALLY NORMAL: YOU DON'T HAVE TO LIVE CRAZY TO FOLLOW JESUS*

Runaway Radical is a heartbreaking, harrowing, but ultimately hopeful story of faith in which twenty-year-old Jonathan Hollingsworth grapples with themes that most people twice or three times his age never ask, or avoid outright. It's a page-turner, too, a who-done-it; one impossible to put down as Jonathan's radically ambitious and impossibly thoughtful efforts are undone by others' avarice and ego. In the end, *Runaway Radical* is a coming-of-age story as moving and meaningful as Salinger, Chabon, or Wolff, in which our young author discovers—and we are reminded—that saving the world often begins right next door.

—BENJAMIN WAGNER, AWARD-WINNING FILMMAKER OF *MISTER ROGERS & ME*

I was gripped by this young man's story; I recognized my story in his. Jonathan, along with his mother Amy, describes the stress put on our kids to be amazing superheroes before they are simply human beings. In Jonathan's case, it was the pressure to be a radical follower of Jesus and sacrificial servant of the church, no matter the cost. This book provides poignant and powerful insights into the pressures on our youth to sacrifice their lives for ideals that aren't always ideal.

—DAVID HAYWARD, AKA NAKEDPASTOR, FOUNDER OF THE LAST SUPPER ONLINE COMMUNITY AND A POPULAR CARTOONIST AND SOCIAL COMMENTATOR

In *Runaway Radical*, Amy and Jonathan Hollingsworth chronicle Jonathan's journey into the depths of a guilt-ridden, you-can-never-do-enough-for-Jesus Christianity and his struggle to find his way back to a genuine gospel where grace and mercy are an experienced reality rather than merely religious words.

—LARRY OSBORNE, AUTHOR AND PASTOR, NORTH COAST CHURCH

With prose that glides like a blade on ice, Amy and Jonathan Hollingsworth have written a film-worthy book that recounts Jonathan's unbridled, if not naive, embrace of the New Christian Radicalism and how that commitment almost destroyed him. *Runaway Radical* is a must-read for anyone who hears the siren song of ministry and mission. However, it is doubly recommended for young adults who have heard the call of Jesus and desire to throw themselves wholeheartedly into following him wherever (they think) he may lead. It is triply recommended for parents who are stunned when the children they raise to follow Jesus actually take them up on it.

—JIM STREET, AUTHOR AND PASTOR, NORTH RIVER COMMUNITY CHURCH, LAWRENCEVILLE, GEORGIA

Amy Hollingsworth is a writer as courageous as she is elegant. Now comes her son, Jonathan, who is the same. Together they guide us into the heart of darkness, a place where misguided yearnings of the spirit often lead. The mother and son then lead us back into the light. I am inspired by the book, and much wiser for having read it.

—TIM MADIGAN, AWARD-WINNING NEWSPAPER JOURNALIST, AUTHOR OF *I'M PROUD OF YOU: MY FRIENDSHIP WITH FRED ROGERS*

More than anything, authors desire to touch the emotions of their audience, but few accomplish this goal. Amy Hollingsworth and her son, Jonathan, have in *Runaway Radical*. From the opening chapter of this grippingly well-written story, the reader gets caught up in the world of Jonathan, as he casts aside creature comforts to serve the Lord on the mission field in Cameroon. Soon disillusioned by the legalism he experiences, we live through Jonathan's pain vicariously, and it's a very familiar feeling. *Runaway Radical* is real, candid, and painstakingly honest—a must-read for anyone who loves the Lord but who has also been wounded by the church.

—JACK WATTS, AUTHOR OF *RECOVERING FROM RELIGIOUS ABUSE* AND BLOGGER AT *PUSHING JESUS*

Amy and Jonathan Hollingsworth recall a haunting account of the enslavement which comes with a new form of legalism—the popularized radical obedience to a gospel which requires sacrifice—to the point of self-harm. With raw and vulnerable honesty, they invite us into their experience with tear-inducing detail and allow us to learn what they have: "the cruelest of paradoxes—that a young man can be both called and led astray." This book is a must-read, not just for those involved in activism overseas and abroad, but for anyone involved in Christianity.

—MICHAEL J. KIMPAN, EXECUTIVE DIRECTOR, THE MARIN FOUNDATION, AUTHOR OF *LOVE NEVER FAILS*

Runaway Radical is provocative in the best sense of the word. It's bold, unflinching, and unswervingly honest to the bone. Amy and Jonathan Hollingsworth have written a book refreshingly free of sentimentality, clichés, and propaganda in any direction. *Runaway Radical* is not only a pull-no-punches critique of the "radical Christian" rhetoric, but a deeply moving human story. The authors are as honest about their own humanity as they are the dark side of the new culture of radical Christian service. As cultural critique, memoir, and a simply beautiful portrait of a relationship between a mother and son, *Runaway Radical* is a startlingly unique genre-bender. It's deeply "radical" in its own way: a daring book of unfiltered, uncompromising grace.

—JONATHAN MARTIN, AUTHOR OF *PROTOTYPE*

Cathartic, powerful, and emotional, *Runaway Radical* reminded me how much of our hard-won wisdom crawls from the ashes of misplaced devotion. You can tell the words were penned while the wounds were still fresh and weeping, and the pages are a salve to the writers *and* the reader. It's part mystery, part biography, part drama, and all cautionary tale.

—JAYSON D. BRADLEY, PASTOR AND BLOGGER

Runaway Radical is a spiritual fist to one's gut. This book begs for an honest dialogue where Jesus has been used, not as the Author of grace, but as a commodity to gain power over others. I have served for over thirty-one years in cross-cultural missions, and I strongly recommend this book for all churches and agencies that send out, and for those who go. *Runaway Radical* is testimony of grace, of the nonnegotiable love a family has for one another. It is an honest dialogue with the God of the universe.

—DR. NIK RIPKEN, AUTHOR OF *THE INSANITY OF GOD*

There is so much to love about *Runaway Radical*, but what I love most is its raw honesty. It's not the cheap honesty that's all the rage today; the kind that's easy to hear and digest because it never really makes us uncomfortable. But it's a genuine, deep, and messy sort of honesty; the sort of honesty an image-obsessed, programming-addicted, got-it-all figured out Church doesn't want to hear, but desperately needs to heed. Whether you're a lifelong believer, a wide-eyed radical ready to save the world, or shepherd with a flock to lead, this book should definitely be on your must-read list.

—ZACK HUNT, BLOGGER AT *THE AMERICAN JESUS*

RUNAWAY RADICAL

A YOUNG MAN'S RECKLESS
JOURNEY TO SAVE THE WORLD

BY AMY HOLLINGSWORTH AND
JONATHAN HOLLINGSWORTH

W PUBLISHING GROUP

AN IMPRINT OF THOMAS NELSON

Published in Nashville, Tennessee, by W Publishing, an imprint of Thomas Nelson.

Published in association with Yates & Yates, www.yates2.com.

Thomas Nelson, Inc. titles may be purchased in bulk for educational, business, fund-raising, or sales promotional use. For information, please e-mail SpecialMarkets@ThomasNelson.com.

In some instances, the names of individuals have been changed.

Library of Congress Cataloging-in-Publication Data

Hollingsworth, Amy.
Runaway radical : a young man's reckless journey and the uncertain fate of a generation bent on doing good / by Amy Hollingsworth and Jonathan Hollingsworth.
pages cm
ISBN 978-0-7180-3123-7 (trade paper)
1. Hollingsworth, Jonathan. 2. Christian converts--United States--Biography. 3. Church work--West, Africa. 4. Radicalism. I. Title.
BV4935.H625H65 2015
277.3'083092--dc23
[B]
2014022319

Printed in the United States of America

15 16 17 18 19 RRD 6 5 4 3 2 1

To my generation, the spiritual runaways:
May we find grace in the things we believe
and peace in the things we don't.
J. H.

CONTENTS

CONTENTS

INTRODUCTION: IS HE REAL?

HE WAS YOUNG ENOUGH TO still be riding in the backseat, not yet tall enough to be in the passenger side up front, next to me. We were alone in the car, arguing about his new older friends in the neighborhood, part of a tough transition to the town we had just moved to. He was embarrassed that his friends saw him leaving the house dressed up every Sunday morning for church since their parents didn't make them go. That's when the questions first began for him.

The questions kept coming—and the answers too, although not as dramatic as what happened that day in the car. Years later, Jonathan would say what he experienced was a panic attack. He'd blurted out the most outrageous thing he could think of to the God of the universe in the presence of his mother, bearing witness, and his eight-year-old body had reacted to his act of rebellion. But he only told that version of the story after he returned from Africa. And everything changed when he returned from Africa. Things shifted; his story got rewritten.

My son says our spiritual paths intersected that day in the car when he asked God if he was real and I had to help carry him from the backseat once we returned home, a limp noodle of a child who had just gotten his answer.

I heave the big suitcase onto the bathroom scale and cross my fingers that it's not more than fifty pounds, the maximum weight for an international flight. The suitcase covers most of the scale, including the numbers, so it's hard to read the verdict. Shifting it only makes the needle dance. I finally get it to balance without my help and lean to the right and then to the left to see if I can make out the numbers. Neither direction will give me an accurate reading, so I straddle the scale until I am directly above it. Forty-five pounds. We made it, with room to spare. Another suitcase goes on the scale.

Jonathan, now a sophomore in college, is leaving for West Africa in the morning. A year's worth of clothes and supplies shoved into two suitcases, carefully calibrated to avoid the hefty fine for overstuffing luggage. Misread the scale, and you pay two hundred dollars.

Across the Atlantic, Jonathan pops in online several afternoons a week to chat, as much as you can chat with an ocean between you. We type messages back and forth, and that's when I realize the honeymoon is over, his idealism washed away by two straight months of rain. Disappointment, culture shock, and lack of sunshine have dissolved his resolve to save the world. These are the only things he confesses at the moment, the only things I know about at the time. It's strange to think how much I fretted

over the scale a few months before. There are more important things you can misread. And pay a steeper price.

Or maybe the instrument itself is off. "I just kept moving
forward, refusing to let go of a broken compass," Jonathan
would say later, having been meticulously prepared to go in
the wrong direction.

Writing things down just after they happen decreases
the margin of error when you try to recall them later on.
Distance muddies accuracy as much as misreading does.
What I remember about that day in the car is my son's
audacity, his very first act of rebellion toward God—or was
it just toward me? It was as if his eight-year-old self, with his
bowl cut and bright eyes, had conjured up the most hurtful
thing he could say to his mother: *How do we even know God
is real?* That's how I remember it now, thirteen years after
it happened.

What Jonathan remembers is that his fear of God—a
literal fear, not a poetic awe—was so strong that he worked
himself into a near heart attack at his own impudence. Other
times he concedes that there might have been a recognition
of God's realness that made him go limp, like a rag doll, but
the awareness was internal, an intellectual leap.

We are both wrong. Because I wrote it down just after
it happened.

The eyewitness accounts were in a cloth box on the top
shelf of my closet. I had to dig through three boxes of journals to find the right one. There it was—October 2, 1999:

Jonathan's Epiphany. That's what I had written at the top of the paper. The story rolled out over four pages, every detail recorded as if I were a cop making an accident report. And the report was clear: it was neither impudence nor panic attack.

The journal entry noted that I had been worried about the change in Jonathan's behavior (that part I remembered correctly). He could be disrespectful; he had been showing off for his older friends. He had just turned eight, and he wasn't the same kid he had been before we moved from our tight-knit community to this new city. (I had the same concerns when he came home from Africa: the child who left was not the same who returned.) But the dustup of preteen rebellion had already settled; the car had emptied of angry words by the time his question had come. We had shifted forward to unravel the great mysteries of the universe, something Jonathan had liked to do. Still likes to do. And then he had asked the question:

"I know I'm going to regret asking this—and I believe in God and everything—but how do we know he's real?"

My journal notes record that we entered into a lengthy discussion about creationism, evolution, general versus special revelation, how the Godhead could be three persons in one, "and other mind-boggling things he asked about." Jonathan was thorough but still unconvinced:

"But how do we *really* know God's real?"

"You shouldn't be afraid to ask God to show you he's real," I told him. We talked for a few more minutes and then sat in silence until we reached our neighborhood. I pulled into the driveway. I turned off the car and turned around. What I wrote in my journal was that Jonathan looked like he had been seized, squeezed tight the way people describe coronaries. His face was pinched, and tears were streaming down his face. I asked him what was wrong. He hesitated to answer; his whole body was shaking.

"He *just* did it! He *just* did it!"

I tried to decipher as best I could.

"He touched me!"

All I could think to say was, "Are you okay? Are you happy—or afraid?"

"Happy!"

I got out of the car and scrambled to get to him. When I opened the door he fell into my arms. He was still in tears; the words came out in vibrato: "I'm s-o-o-o-o h-a-a-a-p-p-y." He put his arms around my neck, his legs buckled, and I half carried, half dragged him to the front door.

One of his new friends, the twelve-year-old, was outside, watching from his front porch.

Inside, I again asked him what happened. He had trouble describing it and continued to cry. "It was the best feeling in the whole world." It was a feeling, an anticipation that something was about to happen—and then this overwhelming sense, as if the God of the universe had touched him. Had answered him.

Jonathan had been overseas before, first a two-week mission trip to France when he was sixteen and then ten days in

Honduras when he was nineteen. France was fun and exciting; Honduras changed him. It was the first time he saw suffering on a large scale, the first time he realized the best efforts of a small group of teens would do little to alleviate it. Of course the food and supplies they carried to the Tolupan Indians were appreciated, but it was a temporary fix. They trudged through the jungles, snapped photos, bought souvenirs, and came home. It wasn't quite spring break, but it wasn't saving the world either.

Two weeks after Jonathan returned, he had a dream, a dream within a dream. He dreamed he was still in Honduras, fast asleep, and that's when the second dream occurred. This one took him out of Honduras, which was in the turbulent throes of its rainy season, and deposited him elsewhere, where it was hot and sunny and tranquil. He was walking through the red dirt streets of a village and came upon a ramshackle hut. There was a mother and a father inside the hut, and a wooden chair outside, close to the road Jonathan was traveling on. Something sacklike had been placed on the chair and as he approached, Jonathan saw that it was a large lump of clay. As he neared the chair, the lump began to shift and crack and pieces of clay fell to the ground, revealing a little African boy underneath. Once emancipated, once enlivened, the child reached out and took hold of Jonathan's arm, cradling it, resting his small head upon it.

Then, Jonathan said, words began to flow from the little African boy, and though inaudible, they relayed a sophistication like those of an adult. Not only the manner of speaking but also the content: it was as if he were looking right through Jonathan, from a place of already knowing. He calmed Jonathan's anxieties; he answered Jonathan's questions before he even asked them. The boy knew what needed reassuring.

Jonathan told me about the dream as soon as he awoke from it. I asked him how the dream made him feel. He had trouble describing it. It must have been the best feeling in the world.

Not a feeling of awe or trembling, but of reassurance and love and understanding. Not an answer to a question, but an anticipation of many questions. The words flowed from the boy in the wooden chair, Jonathan remembers, as from a babe in a manger. A babe made of flesh and blood. Not clay, not spirit.

To a young boy, he showed his power. To a young man, his vulnerability.

Ten months later we packed Jonathan's bags and weighed them on the bathroom scale. The next morning he left for Africa, having been bidden by the clay-cracked boy in the wooden chair.

CHAPTER 1

SACRIFICE

IT HAS ONLY BEEN A FEW DAYS, AND MY HEART IS already exploding with joy.

It has only been a few days, and I already feel at home.

It's amazing what can happen in a matter of days when you're on the other side of the world. Maybe that's what it takes sometimes. From the mansions of politicians to the shacks of humble farmers, I've seen the city and the countryside and everything in between. But everywhere I go I am told the same thing: you are welcome here.

Despite all that has happened since I arrived, the event that stands out to me the most is when I went to the local church Sunday morning to worship. The joyful energy in the room was incredible, and the angelic voices of the children's choir were enough to make me feel like I was worshiping with these wonderful people in the throne room of heaven. I promise, an African church service will ruin you to anything else. When the sermon was over, I was greeted by more people than I could count. The adults showered me with handshakes and hugs. The children greeted me with curious looks, shy smiles, and contagious laughter.

—Jonathan's blog post, written on his third day in
Cameroon, West Africa

For nearly a year Jonathan had agonized over how to save the world. What was his part? What was his purpose? And then within six weeks every detail fell into place. Eight thousand dollars of support were raised in just over a month. Thirty guitars were donated so that he could give African orphans the gift of music, teach them what he had been taught in a privileged youth of weekly music lessons. The newspaper covered his story; his college highlighted his sacrifice. He got all his shots, was granted his visa. The insurance company bent the rules so that he could secure a year's worth of antimalaria medicine. He was prayed over, sent out, chosen. His path was made straight. He aced his last exam of the semester, finished up his thank-you notes, and boarded the plane—all on the same day. We, his happy family—his father, his mother, his sister—cried and hugged him and said good-bye at the airport, never more sure of anything in our lives.

When did you first know things had gone terribly wrong? I asked him months later. About six days in, he admitted. Six days into a yearlong commitment. Just three days after his heart had been exploding with joy.

It was the first morning of a new year, and I made the discovery on Facebook. Someone—most likely the culprit with the shears—had posted before-and-after pictures. I ran upstairs to Jonathan's closet, where he slept on the floor, to find out if it was true. There he was, like a slumbering Samson, shorn of his beautiful mane of curls. He looked like a new recruit, or a cancer patient. Or a monk.

This was not Jonathan's first act of renunciation. His bed was gone, along with most of his bedroom furniture. He slept on the floor of his narrow closet, just long enough to accommodate his six-foot frame. Once he left the house while his meditation candle, the one emblazoned with the image of Our Lady of Guadalupe, still flickered in his closet, and his prayers must have been heard because she spared the house from catching fire. I made a little poster to put on the door, with a smiling friar in cassock and tonsure, with the caption "Brother Jonathan's Cloister Closet." (It was meant to be a joke, especially since the friar had more hair than Jonathan.)

Soon he began to scratch out short messages in pencil on the closet wall, a quote from Mother Teresa or a Bible verse about caring for the poor. Before long he had covered the walls with the words of St. Basil the Great, Mahatma Gandhi, Thomas Merton, Albert Einstein, Che Guevara, Frederick Buechner, Martin Luther King Jr., tragic hero Christopher McCandless, and Jesus himself. It was always a message of self-sacrifice for the sake of others.

I framed a photo and hung it on his closet wall, in the midst of the quotes, when he returned from Honduras. It was a picture of him reaching out his hand to a poor, barefooted Honduran girl. She was tiny for her age, thin and expressionless, with an oversized T-shirt slipping off one shoulder, the applique butterflies muted by dirt. Jonathan noticed that her movements were robotic, as if she didn't have the energy to move fluidly. He knelt down beside her and reached out his hand to her. She stood motionless, looking straight ahead, never acknowledging his presence. He waited. Then slowly, very slowly, she raised her hand and placed it in his. But she never shifted her gaze, her eyes looked straight ahead. Her expression was still blank. But a great change had come over his.

Jonathan was a youth leader at church, and he was asked to speak during a Sunday morning service about his work with the homeless. He wanted to mention how hopeless he felt after seeing the suffering in Honduras, but the pastor edited that part out, asking him to keep things upbeat and positive. After the service, we planned to take Jonathan out to lunch, to celebrate the occasion. He drove on ahead to the restaurant, but when we arrived he was nowhere to be found. We searched inside and out, checked the bathroom. I looked outside a second time and found him behind the building, sitting on the curb near the dumpster. A petite woman sat next to him. Her name was Carmen, and even though the weather was temperate, she was wrapped head to toe in heavy winter clothing.

The next day he told me that a van had stopped in front of him and Carmen as they sat near the dumpster, and a young boy jumped out and handed them each a bag of chips. The boy assumed Jonathan was homeless too. Jonathan's hair was long and curly then, his jeans were ripped, the sole was coming off one of his shoes. And that was his preaching attire.

He and Carmen were old friends by now; he gave her rides from time to time, ran errands for her. He had bought her a luggage cart to transport all her worldly goods when hers was damaged. Sometimes she would ask him to meet her someplace and then not show up.

She had wide, beautiful eyes, but her speech was hard to follow. She wanted to tell me she saw Jesus in the clouds once, or in a rainbow. We invited her to lunch, but she said she was too dirty to go inside. Jonathan thought she was worried about leaving her luggage cart, so we brought her lunch to her. Your son is beautiful, she said.

Later Jonathan admitted, "I felt guilty approaching a homeless person if I hadn't given something up first." So he slept on the floor, shaved his head, broke up with his girlfriend.

Before Jonathan left for Africa, he was invited to the Washington, DC, premiere of the film adaptation of *Blue Like Jazz*. He was one of the thousands of associate producers credited on the film, which boasted one of the largest fundraising efforts in film history. There he met author Donald Miller, shook his hand, and told him: I'm going to Africa because of you.

And it was true. If it hadn't been for that book, which Jonathan had read two years before, he might not have realized his love for others was conditional. He might not have gone to Honduras or held the hand of a little girl or dreamed of a little African boy when he got back. He might

not have started a ministry to reach out to the homeless.
Or met Carmen. He may have never felt he was needed by
the orphans of Cameroon, West Africa. He wrote about the
transformation in a blog post.

> After I finished *Blue Like Jazz*, I felt different, like I was
> walking around with a secret I couldn't contain. The secret
> that everyone matters, everyone deserves love. Suddenly
> no form of human interaction felt too small or insignificant.
> And that's when I started noticing people all around me I had
> been ignoring, people I could be loving but wasn't. I wanted
> that to change. So I reached for the outcasts, the ones
> deemed "worthless" by society. The homeless.

His love for the homeless expanded, extended, and then
he was taking in other outcasts. Mentoring teenage boys
who even the church folk didn't want. The test of love being
to give to those who couldn't give back. Then he saw the
scope of suffering in Honduras. Then he had the dream.

Jonathan had given away most of his material possessions, including his clothes, but there was one thing he
didn't relinquish: his books. He assigned me a list of books
he wanted me to read when he left for Africa, the books that
had paved the way for him to go. Jonathan had always been
deeply affected by literature, had loved books since he was
a little boy. He was only five when he packed up his favorite
books, including his father's boyhood copy of *The Wizard
of Oz*, in a pale blue suitcase that he sealed with duct tape
for good measure. He alerted us that this suitcase was to

go with him should Jesus come back. He could part with everything else but his treasures in heaven had been stored up in the written word, with color illustrations. He would fill a suitcase with books when he left for Africa, too.

I had read *Blue Like Jazz* shortly after he did, at his request. But the new books on his list were different. Less philosophical, more directive. They were filled with the kind of zeal that might fuel an idealistic college student to leave school, to travel alone to a continent he was unfamiliar with, to join forces with people he didn't really know, to stay longer than he should have. But I only figured that out later, after he was already gone, after I began reading the list of books he left behind.

When I missed Jonathan, I sometimes visited his cloister closet. His bedding was still there, unwashed, some blankets and a pillow. That's when I noticed new quotes had been added to the wall. They were less encouraging, more accusatory than the others. Each one issued a challenge. Each one pointed a finger. No longer a wall to inspire, but more like the markings of a prisoner biding his time. Not counting the days to freedom, but further closing him in.

If it was Donald Miller who was responsible for getting Jonathan to Africa, it was these other voices who were responsible for keeping him there. Because there was always more to do. More to give. More to sacrifice. No matter the cost.

I think people are tired of being told about a Jesus they haven't experienced. If someone has never been shown love or peace or mercy, but I claim that Jesus is all of those things, I have done nothing to help that person understand. Instead of just telling people that Jesus loves them, what if I showed them love first? Instead of just saying that Jesus is peace and mercy, what if I showed them what peace and mercy feel like? If I do that, then at last I can say the next part, the most important part: "Friend, the same way I have loved you is how Jesus loves you, and he loves you even more than I can."

This is my journey to make the words of Jesus jump off the page. In three weeks I will be boarding a plane that will take me to Africa for a year to volunteer. I will be teaching orphans and schoolchildren how to play the guitar, traveling to remote villages to do medical outreaches, and helping to build a bakery that will not only teach the orphans a trade but will make the orphanage self-sustaining. This wouldn't be possible without the gracious support of friends, family, and fellow followers of Jesus.

Thanks for loving the world with me.

And so my beautiful son, with a suitcase full of books and a luggage cart transporting all his worldly goods, boarded the plane, poised to love the world.

CHAPTER 2

STORIES THAT DON'T
GET TOLD

ONE OF THE LAST MEMORIES I have before boarding the plane to Africa is standing in front of the painted-on chalkboard that spans an entire wall of my bedroom. This wall bore no literary quotes or Bible verses; it was blank except for a countdown tally that read: DAYS TILL AFRICA.

It was the night before my departure, and the tally needed updating. I erased the previous number, scribbled on the day before, and drew a number one that reached from floor to ceiling. I took a few steps back and let the image sink in. This was a symbolic moment, not only because it represented the beginning of a yearlong trip, but because it represented a trip that I believed would inspire me to stay for good.

I can't count the times a classmate or neighbor told me it wouldn't be surprising if I became so taken with the African culture that I'd never come back. Or, if I did come back, it would be with an orphaned child who I just couldn't bear to part with.

Neither of these predictions came true, of course, and perhaps they were too ambitious for someone who had yet to step foot on the continent. But that didn't stop me from picturing myself in the shoes of every missionary with a success story I'd spent the last two years reading about, wanting to become.

If you are a young, idealistic Christian, then Africa is the place to be. Where else do you find missionaries multiplying loaves and fishes to feed entire orphanages? Or a young woman my age adopting orphaned girls and raising them on her own? Or a nonprofit trying to take down a war criminal? Or people being healed? Or even being raised from the dead?

When Christians tell stories about Africa, they tell stories like these. Every outreach is a success. God always does something amazing. Lives are always changed. Every account is written with the ecstasy of someone whose heart is exploding with joy.

The downside to holding literature so dear is that sometimes you find yourself trying to live out the stories of the characters in your books. This temptation is almost inescapable in Christian literature, where the reader is encouraged, even directed, to view the person as an example to be followed.

As I stared at the countdown on my wall, I had no reason to believe that my story would unfold any differently than the stories of the passionate do-gooders in my books. I had been let down by mission trips before, but those were nowhere near as ambitious as the journey I was about to embark on. If I learned anything from the stories coming out of Africa, it was that if I wanted God's attention, I had to do something big. I had to do something too big for God to ignore. And then, surely then, he would show up. And he would do something amazing.

But the question I never asked myself, the question absent from the countless testimonies I had heard in church, absent from the inspiring accounts of miracles, absent from all the literature urging young Christians to follow God to another part of the world and make disciples, was this: What happens when God doesn't show up?

Where do those stories go? I didn't know the answer then, but I do now. Those stories don't get told. Those stories make God look bad. Those stories make the church look bad.

So they tell you not to tell your story. No newsletter, no slideshow, no testimony. No one is even told you've come home.

Better than a bad story is no story. That way, what happened to you never really happened.

CHAPTER 3

THEY STILL NEED LOVE

TODAY I WALKED THROUGH ONE OF THE NEARBY villages. The winding road was dotted with small houses and crop fields and children pointing and shouting "White man!" as I passed. I entered the thick brush and walked down into a valley. After finding a small clearing, I sat beneath a towering bamboo tree, and in that moment of complete solitude, realized one simple truth: I am here because someone loved me.

I am here because I have been loved deeply by my family and my friends. But the greatest love comes from someone I've never met. I am here because two thousand years ago Someone loved me more than I can ever know. He still loves me, and it would be a shame not to pour out that same love with just as much intensity.

He had gray hair and a white beard and hadn't talked to another living soul in months. He wasn't after company that night; he pulled his camouflage jacket tight against the night air and shuffled past each table at the outdoor restaurant, asking for spare change. It was the spring before Jonathan left for Africa, and he and his friends were sitting outside at their favorite café and hookah lounge when

Bobby Brown made his rounds. He looked like he was in his sixties, someone's grandfather living on the streets.

This was not the first homeless man Jonathan had encountered. Of course he knew Carmen, but she was in the minority, unprotected, which is why he once asked if she could live with us. Most of the homeless in our community, like most communities, were men. The first homeless man Jonathan hoped to help he never got a chance to. A long line at McDonald's, slowed by a new employee in training, held Jonathan up as he attempted to buy the homeless man lunch. If the man knew food was on the way, he might not have abandoned his post on the main thoroughfare. But this was nothing Jonathan had planned. He was driving home from a college class and saw the homeless man limping up and down the median and was seized, squeezed tight, by the urge to buy him lunch, but also to take it to him, and to shake his hand.

While in McDonald's Jonathan met another man who was probably homeless as well. Jonathan remembers the encounter clearly, because he wrote it down just after it happened.

Worn, oversized clothes hung from his scrawny frame, and his skin was weathered from the sun. He was busy counting a pile of change in his hand, when he absentmindedly dropped a few coins on the floor. A penny landed close to my foot. I reached for it and handing it to him, mentioned how every little bit helps these days.

"Sure does," he laughed, revealing several missing teeth.

His eyes were kind, but there was a sort of sweet brokenness about them; they were so compelling I could hardly look away. He inspected the penny I had given to him, and with a smile handed it back.

"You know," he said, "they say when you find a penny heads-up, you have good luck for the rest of the day, so I think you should hang on to this."

Jonathan needed the good luck because the homeless man he intended to help had in fact left his post by the time his order was ready. "I willed him not to go far; if he could only hang on for another few minutes, he could eat." But he didn't hang on, and Jonathan was left to run across the four-lane highway, searching for someone to feed.

It wasn't long before he found him, an old man with a torn cardboard sign and a rusty tin cup, like the kind a prisoner clangs against metal bars when he needs something. He locked eyes with Jonathan from across the busy stretch of road and gleaning his intent, waited patiently for Jonathan to maneuver in and out of traffic to reach him with the white bag of hot food. His hair was a tangled mess under his red baseball cap and Jonathan noticed the tattoos on his forearms, reminders of better days, when they shook hands. What is your name? Jonathan asked. Bond, he answered. B-O-N-D.

Jonathan marked his encounter with Bond as the day that changed his life. A barrier was lifted, a wall torn down, perhaps put there by his well-meaning parents. We gave money to help the local homeless shelter, but were quick to caution our kids against giving money directly to the poor: you never know what they might do with it. Jonathan was ten when we stopped at a traffic light on the way to his guitar lesson, and he handed a homeless man a fresh donut in a paper bag from his window. But the donut had been free with my coffee, so it was a sterile encounter, behind the protection of the glass window, a handing off of something that cost him nothing. Nine years later he would have none of that with Bond: I wanted to feel his handshake. I wanted to know he was real.

Even if some of them proved to be frauds, addicts, or just lazy, Jonathan reasoned that compassion was meant to be unconditional. I had heard that sentiment before, but only in fiction; I didn't know anyone in real life who felt that way. There is an old priest who rebukes a young priest in a classic French novel, and he shares Jonathan's lack of caution, insisting that those who give to the poor shouldn't react in horror when they take the money and instead of spending it on stale bread, go straight to the nearest bar: "A poor man with nothing in his belly needs hope, illusion, more than bread." This is an oft-quoted line from the book, but what the old priest says next is just as important: "You fool! What else is that gold, which means so much to you, but a kind of false hope, a dream and sometimes merely the promise of a dream?"[1]

So Jonathan began taking his promise of a dream and giving it away freely, never caring what happened to it after it left his hands—not the day he met Bond in the middle of traffic or the night he met Bobby Brown at the outdoor café. And for a time, at least, no harm came from it.

You can do things at a distance, like handing over a free donut from inside your car, and you can do things up close. Jonathan had been supporting a little African boy through an international sponsor-a-child program, and it's one thing to have the photos and drawings and report cards sent to you to tack on to the fridge and another thing to have the child touch your face or sit on your lap. Of course it wasn't the exact same child, but children like him, that Jonathan met in Cameroon.

Dozens of children laughing and jumping and hugging and pulling on my arms and legs.

Dozens of children running and shouting "Uncle!" "Uncle!"

Dozens of children holding my hand, and one little girl who wouldn't let go.

Today I visited the school where I'll be teaching music lessons as soon as the guitars cross the Atlantic. I went to ask questions, participate in classes, and get to know the children. The school had a little more in mind.

When I arrived, the woman in charge asked if I could start teaching right away. But I was empty-handed. I didn't have guitars or music books or songs prepared. I had a notepad and about an hour to prepare four lesson plans for four different age groups.

But we made do with what we had. We identified the parts of a guitar on the chalkboard. We learned the names of each string, E B G D A E, which we turned into Every Baby Girl Dances After Eating, a phrase that tickled the children and filled the room with laughter. We practiced our rhythm on air guitars. We learned that sounds are just vibrations, and we proved this by humming and putting our hands to our throats.

When school got out for the day, we played outside in the sun while waiting for the school bus. My white hands were examined by dozens of children, fascinated that they could see the blood in my visible veins. They vigorously wiped my hands "so they could get clean," although I'm pretty sure my hands were dirtier when they were done. I taught them just about every secret handshake I could think of. I gave a million high fives. One of the smaller girls fought the crowd to hold my hand, and once she had it, she wouldn't let it go for anything.

I can't thank God enough for giving me the opportunity to love these children. For giving me a year to watch them learn and grow and worship Him with their new instruments. For letting me do what I was created to do: love.

One of the ways Jonathan learned compassion was from books, and not just from the Good Book, but through literature. (Not every book arms you with a broken compass, leads you astray.) One story especially would have made the cut, certain to be packed away in his duct-taped suitcase bound for heaven. It was the one about Erik, the tortured soul who lived beneath the Paris Opera House, his antics chronicled in Gaston Leroux's famous novel, *The Phantom of the Opera*.

We read the book together when Jonathan was six. In its pages we discovered that the sad saga of the Phantom, the outcast with the disfigured face, was based on actual events. We learned that he was not a monster but a genius, a musical prodigy, an accomplished inventor. We wrung our hands over his unrequited love for opera ingénue Christine Daae, to whom he appeared as an Angel of Music.

We despaired over his thoughtless taking of lives, at the same time recalling that he had lived as a caged animal in a circus freak show. We cried when we read that his mother had rejected him, a fact movingly expressed in the musical: "This face, which earned a mother's fear and loathing; a mask, my first unfeeling scrap of clothing."[2] And then we reached the story's climax, when the Phantom brings Christine to his secret hideaway and his mask falls away and Christine dissolves years of pain with an act of kindness even his mother had refused him: a kiss. It became a lesson indelibly etched in our hearts, a poignant reminder to think twice about playground taunts and unkind words.

Since we had spent so much time getting to know the Phantom, it seemed only fitting that we meet him in person. (We had learned late in the year that the musical was coming to a nearby city the following spring.) With tickets in hand, Jonathan, now seven, and I made the two-hour trek in the rain to the theatre, conveniently located in the middle of a bustling, unfamiliar downtown. We drove around in circles trying to find an empty parking spot. We raced in the freezing rain to the crowded hall where we were to finally meet the man who had become our friend. We made it to our seats with only seconds to spare, due in part to Jonathan's excitement, which required two trips to the bathroom.

With a nod from the conductor, the curtain rose, the chandelier crackled, and the show came alive. Jonathan and I huddled together, whispering our impressions. We peered through binoculars to look at costumes; then closed our eyes to fully absorb the musical splendor of it all.

"It's a true story, you know," Jonathan told the older couple sitting in front of us during intermission. Then he recounted the parts of the story we'd discovered were true—there really was an underground lake in the Paris Opera House, a chandelier really did shatter one night during a performance, killing one, and there's evidence that a mysterious man really lived in the theatre's cellars. That the Phantom was real mattered to Jonathan.

Then much too quickly we were transported to the final scene, where the Phantom stood alone in his underground labyrinth, forsaken by his true love and hounded by a mob thirsty for retribution. When he began to sing what had become his life's sad anthem, "Masquerade, paper faces on parade; Masquerade, hide your face so the world can never find you,"[3] I looked over at Jonathan. A single tear was streaming down his face. It surprised me that at his age he could tap into the emotions of such a complex character, that he could understand what isolates a person and causes a lifetime of pain. Maybe it was then, as the cymbals clashed and the stage darkened, that he learned to love the outcast.

It was another time our spiritual paths intersected, another time I was there to witness and write down the things that would impel Jonathan to save the world.

THEY STILL NEED LOVE

One of the first questions Jonathan was asked when he arrived in Cameroon is why Americans are so taken with African children. "African children are just different," Jonathan told them. "The kids here are trusting; they'll run up to you and throw their arms around you, even if they don't know you." The longer Jonathan was in Africa, the more he saw this affection as arising from a sense of community, everyone looking out for everyone else. You can talk to a stranger if you know the other adults in the community are keeping close watch.

> It makes me sad that there are people in the States who do bad things to children. And I know this makes parents fearful, but it also makes them overreact.

He might have been thinking of his own parents, whose caution against the homeless extended to any stranger, whose protective shield proved to be an illusion.

> It makes me sad that we let people get so lonely, so disconnected that they stop looking at others as human beings. It makes me sad that a man can hide inside the four walls of his house and plot all kinds of horrible things and his next-door neighbor is oblivious because they live in their own private worlds, even if those worlds are separated by the same fence.
>
> I say all this because for the first time in my life, I'm experiencing a culture that embraces community. Neighbors cook together and wash laundry together. Doors stay open

and people are always passing through for a warm meal or a place to sleep. In this community we live together and laugh together and learn from each other.

I think people were meant to live in this kind of community. To live without others is dehumanizing and it makes us lost and confused and we forget who we are and that our neighbor is somebody too. Perhaps it is not surprising why so many people are so screwed up. But I don't think they are crazy, or even that they are bad people. I think they are just people who lost their community somewhere along the way.

"You get more chances to help people than anyone I know," Jonathan's now former girlfriend once told him. It was true the day he met Bond, and it was true the night he met Bobby Brown. Jonathan and his friends invited Bobby to eat with them, and he traded in his expectation of pocket change for a hot meal. He was quiet at first, content to listen in on the chatter of close friends. But then Bobby began to loosen up, telling stories that made the entire table of young people laugh.

"You folks are nice people, real nice people," Bobby admitted. "I think my son would like you all. I wish you could meet him."

Jonathan didn't know why Bobby wasn't living with his son; he offered Bobby his phone to call him, but his son never picked up. When Bobby fell back into quiet, Jonathan tried to draw him out. He was sitting next to Bobby, which made it easier to start a private conversation, to get him talking again. That's when he learned about Bobby's health issues, that he had asthma and had been in the hospital with a broken arm or a bum leg recently. Bobby told him that he had once encountered a bear in the woods. That he was going on welfare and would have a decent apartment soon. (Jonathan later found out that never happened.) That a few months before he had been robbed at knifepoint by another homeless person at the campsite where many of the street people lived. That's what drove him out of community. He set up a pallet in the woods behind a gym, alone, to protect himself. He leaned close to Jonathan: "I been staying low for three months. Been by myself all that time. Ain't talked to no one." He hadn't talked to another human being—except to beg for money—in three months.

Jonathan couldn't imagine going three hours without talking to someone.

When the evening ended, Jonathan drove Bobby back to the woods behind the gym; Bobby didn't think twice about sharing the whereabouts of his secret hideaway, tucked away like the Phantom's invisible lair. He trusted Jonathan, and together, at least for that night, they formed a new community. Jonathan gave him the sleeping bag he kept in his truck. "I love you, man, and none of that fake crap," Jonathan told him as they said good-bye.

"I love you, too," Bobby said. Sated with food and conversation, and having let down his mask, Bobby took the sleeping bag and slipped off into the woods.

Jonathan never saw Bobby Brown again, but he took that experience with him to Africa; in fact, he went to Africa in part because of that experience. What he learned that night is that Bobby Brown didn't need him sleeping on the floor of his closet or giving away his earthly possessions as a show of solidarity. More than identification, even more than money, Bobby Brown needed his company. Bobby Brown needed his presence. Not just community with someone, but with someone he trusted.

> Today I was thinking about how Americans go to foreign countries and fall in love with the local children. And really, it makes sense. Who wouldn't fall in love with children who are always so happy to see you, who run to you every time you're near, who clamor to get on your lap and snuggle, even though they barely know you? We hold them; we take pictures with them. We thrive on their laughter.
>
> But let's not kid ourselves. What is there to lose? How difficult is it, really, to love a bunch of children who are going to hug you and kiss you and love you right back? Is it really that self-sacrificial to love someone when you know that love will be reciprocated? How much greater to love the unlovable, those who are not going to appreciate it, who won't love you in return?
>
> We were at a crusade tonight in one of the villages, and all these thoughts were going through my mind, that loving these children is such a safe bet, how it doesn't really challenge our hearts, how we probably enjoy all the attention just as much as they do. But then I looked over in the corner where all the kids were sitting on a mat on the ground, and despite my wariness of the whole "American bonding with

random African children" cliché, God urged me to go sit with them anyway. It was almost as if He was telling me, "Of course they're easy to love. But they still need love."

I think this goes for both groups of people. The people who won't appreciate our love are the ones who need it just as much as the ones who will appreciate it. And the people who will love us back need just as much love as the ones who won't.

Maybe we're just meant to love the person in front of us. That way we are not picking and choosing; we are just doing. Sometimes it's easy, like loving the kid in the corner with the cute smile. Other times it's not so easy, like loving the drunk in the corner who's mumbling to himself. Sometimes the person in front of us is a grandfather living on the streets, who hasn't spoken to another living soul in months. Whoever it may be, the answer is the same. Whoever they are, they still need love.

Jonathan had been home from Africa for five months. He didn't return to college; he didn't go back to his old church. He didn't get many chances to help people either, his girlfriend's words now ringing hollow. He stopped serving food at the homeless shelter; he stopped buying lunch for people peddling on the streets. No more rides for Carmen. The wall that had been torn down was now back up. And then one night, when he was heading into a bookstore to buy *Walden*, a book about living in solitude, apart from community, a man emerged from the rain and darkness and stopped him. "Hey," he said, "I think you've helped me before."

The man explained that he and his family were locked out of the homeless shelter where Jonathan had served, either it was too late in the evening or there were no vacancies. They needed money for a place to stay and for food. "I could use your help again," he said.

Now there was a person in front of Jonathan. Perhaps, despite the driving rain, the smoldering candle would flicker back to life.

Not because Jonathan was willing to once again empty his pockets, though he did. But in doing so, he was conceding something far more important: that he still knew, that he still believed in, what he was created to do.

CHAPTER 4

ASHIA

WHEN I HAD THE CHANCE to slip out on my own in Africa, I would take walks around the village and spend time with the locals. The mission organization had always encouraged me to go out and meet people, but only as an opportunity to evangelize. As long as I established boundaries, as long as I kept my distance and didn't get too involved, as long as my interactions were short, sweet, and sterile, I was relatively free to mingle with whomever I chose.

In Cameroon, there is a very cut-and-dried distinction between the church folk and the nonchurch folk. Smoking and drinking are unquestionably sinful behaviors for any Cameroonian who considers himself a real Christian, so you would never see a believer frequenting the bars or lighting up on the streets. But this dividing line never made sense to me; I couldn't see how these forbidden acts were indicative of anything, really. So when I was invited to bars, I drank. When I was offered a smoke, I didn't turn it down.

In many ways, the community I discovered at the bars and on the streets began to feel more authentic than the community I found at church, and the cigarettes and the beer felt more authentic a communion than bread and wine. It was never my place to correct or convert. If anything, I was meeting a need I saw both in myself and in the people around me, and that was the need for togetherness.

One evening, a young man stopped me outside the convenience store and asked if I could bum him a smoke. I asked him about himself, about what he did for a living and what he studied when he was in school. I learned that his girlfriend had passed away a month before, and now he was living by himself and trying to figure out what to do with his life. He asked what I was doing in Cameroon. "Are you a missionary?" he asked. I never liked that term, but the simple answer was yes. He paused to watch me take a drag of my cigarette, but whether or not he observed any sort of contradiction, he held his tongue.

What about you? I asked. Do you go to a church or anything? He grinned sheepishly and explained that he'd been to church a few times, but that it wasn't really for him. He seemed at a loss for words, and then motioned toward the cigarette in his hand. "I like to smoke, you know. I like to drink; I like to sex, you know." His voice trailed off again, and he laughed. I knew what he was getting at, and it was an attitude I had become familiar with from those on the outskirts, from those who didn't adhere to the rigid code of conduct laid down by the African church culture.

I had witnessed the same attitude in a farmer several weeks prior while I was taking a walk through the rural section of the neighborhood. Like the man outside the convenience store, the farmer was curious about what brought me to Cameroon. Our conversation went much the same way, and I asked him if he had any religious affiliation as well. "Oh no," he said, shaking his head dismissively. "I'm not a Christian. I mean, l talk to God sometimes, and I like reading the Bible, but I haven't been to church in a long time."

We were in the middle of nowhere, out of earshot of anyone nearby, and I said something I wouldn't have dared to say in a church or around the people in my mission agency. Don't let anyone tell you that you're not a Christian because you're not going to church, I lamented. God doesn't care about that. He just wants a relationship with you.

I said something similar to the man outside the convenience store, and though he understood what I was saying, though he nodded his head while I spoke, he still looked unconvinced. The farmer, on the other hand, walked away grinning ear to ear, like I'd just told him the most incredible thing he'd ever heard.

Sooner or later word got back to the mission agency that I had been spotted smoking in the neighborhood, and I was told my behavior was unacceptable. While I was being berated by the head of the organization, all I could think of was the farmer and the man who'd lost his girlfriend, but I didn't say anything. I was told that under no circumstances was I allowed to smoke or drink during my stay, and I was to stop immediately because it sent a bad message. It was destructive, it threatened the reputation of the mission agency. And that was that.

There is an expression in the native language of Cameroon that people use to encourage one another, to express sympathy during unfortunate circumstances. The word is *ashia*, which translates simply as "I'm sorry," or "[have] courage." But there is a third, more nuanced meaning of *ashia* that implies a shared struggle. It is less about one person consoling another, but an acknowledgment of solidarity between two people experiencing the same pain.

For example, when two people are caught in the same storm and pass each other on the street, one might say *ashia*, to which the other would nod and say *ashia* back. They are not so much acknowledging the inconvenience, the way I might say "this sucks" to a passenger in the airport when we find out our flight has been delayed. Rather, *ashia* is more about the bond that shared circumstances creates between two people. It's like saying, "We are together."

What I had with the homeless and the Cameroonians was *ashia*. I hadn't lost the woman I loved, and I hadn't been estranged from the church, but like those people, I was lonely. I was in a foreign country, without friends or family, working for an organization that was slowly tightening its grip on me, in more serious ways than whether I smoked or drank. I was living in a Christian culture that unashamedly drew a line between themselves and the outside world. We each had our separate stories, we had our reasons for our loneliness, but in our loneliness is where we found *ashia*. In our loneliness, we were together.

CHAPTER 5

DOES HE SEE?

BEFORE I LEFT FOR AFRICA, PEOPLE BACK HOME ASKED
me if I had any fears about going. At the time I said no, but
I am starting to think I spoke too soon. I am not afraid of
disease. I am not afraid of running out of food or clean water.
My biggest fear is not something tangible.

It is not something that can hurt the body.

It is something that can hurt the soul, and that's what
scares me the most.

My biggest fear is that I will fail to give God the glory he is
due. Especially when I see the people around me and realize
I don't give him nearly as much as I should. I'm afraid I will
get caught up in doing something "noble," that somehow I will
think I can do great things. Mother Teresa said, "We cannot do
great things, only small things with great love."

I want to be like the people of West Africa. Lord, help me
to do small things with great love. *Your* great love.

I give you all the glory.

Jonathan reached across the front seat and took hold of my
hand. *Our spiritual experiences seem to take place in cars,* I
thought to myself. Or in this case a truck. It was his turn in the
driver's seat. We were en route to the lab for follow-up blood

work, and sensing my distress, he reached out for my hand. His solace made me think of one morning when I was pregnant with Emily and emotionally volatile; I slumped down on the edge of the bed and began to cry, my head falling into my hands. Jonathan was barely two, but he ran over to me and with his little fingers tried to lift my head, certain that I would be unable to cry if my head were upright. "No!" he cried out, pushing my head up, up, up. He thought he could keep me from pain. I wanted to cry that day in his truck too, cover my face with my hands, but I didn't want to hurt him. There are times when a son can't help but break his mother's heart.

There were repercussions from Africa we knew about, the malnutrition and the depression. Recently we had learned of thyroid problems and vitamin D deficiency from months without sun. But the doctor suspected another issue, either something he was exposed to in Africa or just as likely a consequence of some reckless behavior once home. That's why we were on our way to the lab that day. Jonathan had gone in the opposite direction, excess being the converse of asceticism. He had reason to be afraid of something that could hurt his body.

"I know I'm going to regret saying this," he said, squeezing my hand, his words reminiscent of another time alone in the car together, "but I think God hates me."

The idea that a person's physical safety is inconsequential in light of eternity came from one of the books Jonathan read before he left for Africa. The deeper the relationship with

Jesus, it promised, the more danger you'll encounter. And then, of course, if you are often in mortal danger, others can assume your special proximity to Jesus. Danger as a badge of honor, as the mark of a true disciple.

Since his return from Africa, Jonathan has been anxious to paint over his cloister closet, to cover up his wall of misdirection, but for now I've asked him to let the quotes stand, as witnesses, as scars. The books themselves, though, he has banished from the house, the same way I had to get rid of all my *Seventeen* magazines when I was in college, lest the eating disorder come back.

Jonathan faced physical danger in Honduras, though not on purpose and not as a way to gauge his commitment to Christ. Torrential rains caused flooding in the Tolupan village where the young missionaries were serving, making it impossible for them to come home. The small group of teenagers spent the day building a bridge over the ground gutted by the downpour, and while they crossed the bridge successfully, the stream on the other side was swollen, impassable. They had to turn back.

They had worked all day building the bridge, but there was no water to replenish them. They only had food for a few days, and it could have taken weeks for the water to recede. (What Jonathan didn't fear in Africa actually happened a year before in Honduras.) Two days later and with supplies nearly exhausted, the mission team had no choice but to make another attempt. They were able to cross the stream, but only "by the skin of our teeth," Jonathan remembers. Their narrow escape came on the heels of a prophecy, foretold by the team leader's wife, that one of the young people would not make it home; he or she would be killed during the course of the mission. That night they stayed in a hostel without running water or electricity, and within a few days transferred to a hotel where they were safe and warm.

The village's problems were not so easily remedied. Most likely the entire season of crops, which the young people had helped weed with machetes the day the rain started, was completely lost. The Indians couldn't take on a second job to make ends meet; they had no backup plan for their subsistence. They lived in the middle of nowhere. And it was that reality—and not the perilous escape—that posed the real danger for Jonathan; it was something that could hurt his soul. For the first time in his life he wondered if God really saw the suffering in the world. Not the danger he experienced for a few days, but the lifetime of weariness for the Indians he left behind. For the little barefooted girl with the oversized T-shirt and muted butterflies who had, at last, offered him her hand.

When he returned, his sadness was palpable. One day he came into my home office while I was writing and began to cry. He was shaken, he wasn't sure God really saw the hurting of the world. The list seemed endless: Who would provide clean water? Who would stop human trafficking? Who would rescue child soldiers? The uncertainty propelled him into a crisis of faith. He began to view his free time, a summer off from college classes and a part-time job, as an indictment of his complacency. How do I reconcile my comfortable life with the plight of the Tolupan Indians? Even the cool summer rain was a haunting reminder of ruined crops, impending starvation.

He felt lost. He needed direction. He wondered if he had the physical and emotional strength to go on. The prophecy about loss of life, unwisely divulged to a group of teens, proved false, unless you count Jonathan, who was a spiritual casualty. The needs were overwhelming in this one little village, this one small part of the world—and he was unable to help even them. And isn't it God who says to the rain shower, "Be a mighty downpour"? (Job 37:6b). That only added to his confusion.

The first question he had ever asked of God was, "Is he real?" Now he would ask, "Does he see?"

He went searching for answers. What he found—in the sharp words of authors challenging him to lose his life for the sake for others—was that it was up to him to see and relieve the suffering in the world. It was also possible that it was his fault there was suffering in the world in the first place, an imbalance created by his middle-class life of privilege.

He could sit and despair, or he could go and do something about it.

Going and doing required some preparation, according to Jonathan's new sources. First, he needed to feel deep guilt, given that his life of leisure put others in great need. Next, he needed to absolve himself of that guilt by living, at least outwardly, in a way that showed he was trying to balance the economic injustices of the world. And lastly, he needed to point a finger at anyone else who wasn't living as he was.

This is how the world was to be saved. You are now baptized in the name of guilt, in the name of sacrifice, in the name of self-righteousness. Now off you go to make disciples.

Jonathan's sadness melded into something more akin to confident misery, confident because he was sure he had the right answer and misery because that's the fruit of trying to outdo yourself every new day. He went from humble monastic to Old Testament prophet. He expected those around him to meet the same impossible standards, challenged them to make the same sacrifices. His concern for the suffering made him insufferable. Although lauded as new and radical, the message in the books was anything but original, anything but revolutionary. Many of the same ideas had infiltrated Christendom for centuries. It was Basil the Great, an ancient bishop, who nearly seventeen hundred years ago issued the same directives, under the same guise: compassion for the poor:

> When someone steals another's clothes, we call them a thief. Should we not give the same name to one who could clothe the naked and does not? The bread in your cupboard belongs to the hungry; the coat unused in your closet belongs to the one who needs it; the shoes rotting in your closet belong to the one who has no shoes; the money which you hoard up belongs to the poor.

Basil the Great, dusted off, polished, and repackaged for the bestsellers' list, shiny and new and poised to jolt the Starbucks generation out of their complacency. Basil the Great, whose words I found scratched on the wall of Jonathan's closet after he left for Africa. The message shifted from admonition to accusation: It's not simply that you aren't doing enough. It's that you are stealing. You are no different than a thief. Or worse. If a child starves while you are well-fed, noted one author, you may even be a murderer.

Jonathan played Jesus in the passion play at church and then ruined Easter dinner by condemning our family for planning a vacation. His coats and shoes were gone; now he was after ours. Even the meal at the restaurant was an extravagance. That money could have been given to the poor, he said. But the Jesus he had just portrayed had the same complaint leveled at him when he allowed Mary to bathe his feet in expensive perfume. Jesus saw through the disciples' guise of compassion, took the opportunity to soften the hardness that underlay the accusation. He answered their question by redirecting their concern. "The poor you will always have with you," he told them, "but you will not always have me" (Matthew 26:11). It was as if Jesus were saying: let Mary love the person in front of her.

Jonathan began to pray that God would pass him over, would allot his blessings to others. He said that the first twenty years of his life had been so blessed that he could be miserable for the rest of his life and still be grateful. Should God feel compelled to bring Job-like suffering upon him, he said, he only asked to be steeled against the blow.

Impending doom is another tenet of the new literature that had captured Jonathan's heart and mind, suffering being the corollary to danger as an indicator of closeness to Christ. A positive example of impending doom was Job, who despite all his suffering, never gave in to the temptation to curse God. Danger was illustrated by a negative example, an anti-hero, the rich young ruler who wouldn't give up his riches to follow Christ, wouldn't relinquish his worldly possessions to gain eternal life. He is every American Christian, the books proclaim, too tied to comfort and safety to be a true disciple. The rich young ruler is the devil in all of these books, Jonathan said, the kind of person they warn you about. You didn't want to be him. You had to do everything possible to avoid being him.

And so he winnowed his life down to the bare necessities. Soon sleeping on the floor of his closet wasn't enough; he had to empty its contents. It wasn't just about skipping a four-dollar coffee; he had to simplify his entire diet. Even his work with the homeless took on a new dimension: he made a pledge that if someone asked him for money, he would hand over whatever was in his wallet at the moment, whether it was two ones or two twenties. Once he had shaved his head as an act of renunciation. Now he would grow it back and refuse to cut it—a requirement of the Nazarite vow taken by the likes of Samson and John the Baptist—for the same reason. How is it that long hair and no hair could be equally pleasing to God? It didn't matter, because new rules were added daily.

In Jonathan's thinking, his self-denial served a two-fold purpose. First, it kept him detached from the things that slipped up the rich young ruler. He didn't want to miss

God's call by being too comfortable, so he purposely made himself uncomfortable. He began to erase his attachment to the life he loved. And second, it prepared him for the worst-case scenario should he be called to suffer as Job did. Serious servants of God were tested. They were called upon to give more, do more, endure more. Didn't Mother Teresa have deformed feet because she constantly chose to wear the worst pair of shoes donated to her ministry? He had to prepare for the ultimate test.

"I didn't fast in order to pray," Jonathan remembers. "I fasted to learn how to starve."

The promise of doom produces fear, and the fear becomes a superstition, a false prophecy, like the one that scares a group of teens in the Honduran jungle. Sometimes it becomes a different kind of prophecy, a self-fulfilling one. "I don't want to miss God's call, but even more important, I don't want to fail his test," Jonathan said. "No matter what happens, I never want to curse God."

Two months after he returned from Honduras, Jonathan had a car accident in nearby Richmond. His truck had been towed, and he was sitting on the ground waiting for a ride home. He had just come from a political rally where he had been pushed and spit on. He was on his way to buy a documentary to show that evening to encourage the troops of his newly formed Youth for Social Justice. Then he had the car crash.

He sat in the hot summer sun, nauseated by hopelessness.

The questions began to run through his head again: Does God really see the suffering in the world? His eye is on the sparrow, but who is watching over these invisible people, the ones we have to walk through the jungle to get to? The ones we had to build a bridge to leave behind?

He had reason to ask these questions. He had saved up a thousand dollars to go back to Honduras, to work in an orphanage and to serve the Tolupan Indians again. He knew then, sitting alone on the side of the road, that his money would have to go to repairs instead. In fact, it cost him every penny he had saved in the two months since he returned. He was being stopped, dramatically, from righting a wrong, from fulfilling his desire to go back and redeem his uselessness in Honduras.

At that moment of both recognition and despair, he heard these words in a whisper, received the answer to his questions: "Blessed are those who mourn, for they will be comforted" (Matthew 5:4). It felt like a promise.

It wasn't a promise that every need would be met or that every ruined crop would be restored. It wasn't a promise that the Tolupans would never know hunger. But it was a promise that those who mourn, those who grieve, those who know hardship would be comforted. It was an answer to his despair. Not a complete answer, but an honest answer.

Perhaps all God was asking of him was to comfort those who mourn. The despair lifted. God had crashed Jonathan's plans to go to Honduras, but in its place had offered him a simple assurance. He had heard Jonathan's concerns about the poor, just as Jesus had heard the disciples'. He took the opportunity to soften the hardness that underlay the accusation. He answered Jonathan's question by redirecting his concern: comfort those who mourn.

For the first time since he returned from Honduras, Jonathan had peace. He had hope. It was the best feeling in the world.

Jonathan knew what it meant to comfort those who mourn. In many ways Carmen and Bond and Bobby Brown had all been mourning—broken relationships, wasted opportunities, hurtful experiences like being robbed by one of your own. And Jonathan was the kid his friends always came to when they needed to unburden their souls. But this day was different. It was the Wednesday before Thanksgiving, and Jonathan received a garbled text message from a friend. Worried, Jonathan called his friend, who sounded sleepy and confused on the other end of the phone. Jonathan drove to his home, and when Mike met him at the car, Jonathan could tell he was altered, almost in a trance.

Jonathan prodded and his friend finally conceded, "I took too many sleeping pills."

"How many?" Jonathan asked.

"I don't know, maybe thirty," his friend said.

"Why?"

"To end it," his friend admitted.

Jonathan knew that his friend had taken two or three sleeping pills before to fight insomnia, but never this many. Mike began to hallucinate. Jonathan began to panic. He tried to get some food in Mike and then rushed him to an urgent care center, but his friend wouldn't leave the car. Jonathan ran inside to alert the staff, and an attendant followed him back to the car with a wheelchair.

Mike sneered at Jonathan and threatened to punch him.

The medical personnel ran some tests. The doctor wasn't sure how Mike was still alive; it was as if his body was in the throes of a heart attack. Mike was rushed to the emergency room with Jonathan riding shotgun in the ambulance. For the rest of the day Jonathan sat by himself in the waiting room as family came and went, watched as a stoic grandfather was reduced to tears.

Once out of medical danger, Mike was transferred to a mental health facility. We didn't know anything of his suicide attempt until late that night when Jonathan returned home. He never called to ask our advice during the course of the day; he just moved on instinct, did what he thought was best. We had to spend Thanksgiving out of town with family, and on Friday, Jonathan went to the facility to see Mike, bringing him a book of Bukowski's poetry as a gift. But the visiting hours had been truncated because of the holiday, and they wouldn't let Jonathan in.

He went back to his truck, book in hand, and began to cry. His friend could have killed himself; he could have gotten behind the wheel of a car and killed others. Nothing was going to jar him awake, not even a car crash. Jonathan felt so helpless, so hopeless. Does God really see the suffering in the world? His eye is on the sparrow, but who is watching over Mike?

If he had listened very closely, he may have heard: I am, which is why I put him in front of you.

It's easy now to see which voice Jonathan should have listened to. But God's answer to the suffering of the world—a
promise to comfort those who mourn—seemed quaint,
simple. It didn't put Jonathan in danger; it didn't cost him
anything. It didn't require him to move to the inner city or
make his own clothes. It wasn't dramatic or extreme. He
knew what it was like to save a life, perhaps many lives if
Mike had not been taken to the hospital, if Mike had tried
to drive himself.

But that wasn't enough. Jonathan had to save the world.
Because the world was full of suffering. Some suffering
was external, like rain that destroys a season of crops and
starves out a village. Some suffering was internal, like pain
that propels a friend to take too many sleeping pills. And
some suffering was needless, the product of false prophecy,
the result of misdirection.

It's not just the suffering of self-denial that is needless;
it's pretend suffering, to do without a bed or proper shoes
may be a show of solidarity, but it doesn't change much.
It doesn't even prepare you for the ultimate test because
the truth is, no one passes that test. There is always more
you can do; there is always more you can give. And when
you fail, and you will, you end up in despair. You begin to
do things that might harm your body and your soul, not
because you want to please God but because you no longer
care to. Not because you want to give God all the glory, but
because you want to curse him.

That's what was unspoken that day Jonathan and I were
on our way to the lab for his blood tests. It wasn't just that

he feared God hated him; he feared he hated God. When he failed to meet impossible standards, he doubted God would ever be satisfied. And he stopped trying, he reversed direction, he brought suffering on himself. He self-medicated, he self-destructed. He became his own impending doom.

In his attempt to avoid becoming the rich young ruler, he had become the prodigal.

CHAPTER 6

A DIRTY MIRROR

AS IT TURNED OUT, LEAVING American Christianity behind did not solve all my problems. In fact, I was beginning to see that my frustrations with Christianity were not unique to America at all. The grass was not greener in Cameroon, and that is because the grass is not greener anywhere. I could travel country to country, jumping from one spiritual movement to the next, and still not find a practicing religion that hadn't been tainted in some way.

I had traveled halfway around the world only to learn I was running in circles.

When I first stepped foot in Cameroon, I only saw what I wanted to see. The idea of Africa as a spiritual utopia was so ingrained in my mind that any evidence to the contrary just didn't register. So I explained away the misogyny. I made excuses for the prosperity teachings and the false prophecies. Anything that didn't sit right with me I chalked up to cultural differences. And this arrangement worked seamlessly, for a time.

But there came a point where I could no longer deny the reality of the situation. The Cameroonian church system was more corrupt than I could have imagined, and I had just pledged the next year of my life to promoting it and supporting it. I was slowly coming to terms with an unpleasant truth about Africa, but in the process, I would also learn an unpleasant truth about myself.

Abstaining from drink and smoke was just the tip of the iceberg when it came to the Cameroonians' efforts to win favor from God. Cameroonians feel poor and powerless, so naturally the brand of Christianity they've adopted is one that promises wealth and power. And on the surface, it seems to work. One look at almost any established Cameroonian pastor will confirm this. He is impeccably dressed, drives a nice car, and sometimes his office is even furnished with a flat screen TV and a much-coveted air-conditioning unit. Women wait on him hand and foot; he is a king. So when a pastor stands behind the pulpit and promises the untold riches of a life in Christ, people buy it; after all, his lifestyle speaks for itself. That's why so many young men are desperate for their own churches. With perks like that, who wouldn't want to be a pastor?

I was living in a country of arm-twisters. The religious men twisted the arms of the women in order to be served. They twisted the arms of the congregation, urging them to tithe, promising that God would see their sacrifice and return the blessing sevenfold, when all the while the pastor is decorating his home with the pennies of widows. The leaders of my organization and many others like it were twisting the arms of their volunteers, squeezing money out of them and their supporters, using them like puppets for publicity. But worst of all, these men were twisting, and teaching their followers to twist, the arm of God.

The question of what can I do for God had brought me here, but the only question being asked now was what can God do for us?

I believed everything I had read about experiencing the heart of Jesus in the poor. But now I was with the poor, and I didn't recognize Jesus's face in theirs. I recognized the Bible thumpers and megachurch swindlers from my own country. Their fervent prayer no longer brought me joy; it made me sick. Their cries no longer felt authentic, but theatrical.

But the more I uncovered about Cameroonian church culture, the more I uncovered about myself. Everyone warned me about culture shock, how different things would be. But the real shock was how similar things were. And it took the exaggerated example of the Cameroonians for me to see that.

What connected me to the Cameroonians was not necessarily the things we sought God for, but the methods we used to obtain them.

As much as I justified my own beliefs, as much as I told myself that I was different, that surely my pursuit of experiencing God was nobler than pursuing his blessings, I realized that I was using God just as much as they were. Money and blessing were their commodity; mine was trying to get God's attention, to win his approval.

Helping others was my form of self-help. I didn't ask God for money, but I was still asking him, begging him, twisting his arm for something that would make my life complete.

And maybe that is why I continually flung myself into the unknown, intentionally putting myself in situations that would test my faith and risk my health—I thought I could force God's hand. I thought that by making a spectacle of myself, I could get him to act. I could get him to notice me and the people around me. I was the kid in the pool pretending to drown so the lifeguard would save him.

At the time, I didn't realize the extent of what I was doing. I didn't realize that my acts of sacrifice were nothing more than attempts to summon God, to win his trust and approval. Before the trip was over, I would pull more and more of these stunts, but the outcome was always the same.

I was holding up a cloudy lens through which I viewed the Cameroonians pulling their theatrics, trying to harness God. But if I had taken the time to wipe the glass, I would've seen my own reflection. That's when I realized it wasn't a glass but a mirror. I was not looking out. I was looking in.

CHAPTER 7

THE LAST SACRED PLACE ON EARTH

BEFORE WE LEFT THE STATES, PETER, THE HEAD OF THE mission organization I'm working with, mentioned that my schedule here would be flexible, that I would be free to pursue my interests and follow the Lord wherever he may lead me.

At the time, I couldn't have imagined all the possibilities before me now. In addition to teaching music to children at the school and the orphanage, I can teach computer classes at the cyber café, lead worship at church, help small business owners apply for microfinance loans, minister on talk-radio programs, counsel patients at the medical center, or even just take the day off to play soccer with the children in the villages. Opportunities to help the community are available everywhere I turn. It seems I will have my hand in a little bit of everything.

Today we took a trip to one of the villages. Far from the hustle and bustle of the city, paved roads turned into paths of red dirt framed by lush greenery and the looming Mount Cameroon. Despite the beauty of the surroundings, evidence of dire poverty is all around. I witnessed what is typical of rural areas in Cameroon: house after house constructed out of no more than mud, wooden planks, and sheet metal.

As I walked through the village, my surroundings came

> to life as dirty, poorly dressed, beautiful children came out of
> hiding to smile and wave and giggle at the white man walking
> down the road. Despite all the incredible things I've seen so
> far, this place has captured my heart the most. If it's up to me,
> I'll be spending quite a bit of my time here.

It was his fifth day in West Africa and Jonathan was roaming a red dirt street dotted with ramshackle huts on a hot and sunny and tranquil day. His surroundings came to life because children came to life, sneaking out of hiding to see the white man traveling on their road. No wonder his heart was captured, no wonder he wanted to spend all his time there. He had dreamed of this scene, sleeping on the floor of his closet, just after his return from Honduras. The clay-cracked boy had multiplied, and now Jonathan was being embraced by a village full of beautiful African children.

The list of possibilities had grown. The newspaper account previewing Jonathan's year overseas listed all the things he would be doing while there: teaching guitar lessons, establishing a digital record-keeping system for a medical clinic, constructing a church, and building a bakery for the orphanage. Once he arrived in Africa, there were even more opportunities to serve.

Jonathan was the first long-term volunteer for a fledgling mission organization run by a native of West Africa now living in the States. Word of Jonathan's commission—with headlines like "College on Hold for Cameroon" and "Helping Humanity Trumps Textbooks"—brought in lots of money for the organization, led to lots of publicity. "He's going to be pretty busy," Peter, the head of the mission organization, told our local reporter, adding that Jonathan's drive to serve others gelled perfectly with his group's mission. "We're happy to just be a bridge he can cross to reach his dream." Jonathan was happy too.

> I've spent the better part of the last year studying social justice. But now I want to know the faces behind the statistics of poverty, the statistics of AIDS. I want to get up-close, to see the face of Jesus. Mother Teresa said, "In the poor we find Jesus in his most distressing disguise." What we do for the least of these, we do for him.
>
> My excitement to love the world also comes with a profound sense of sadness. I get discouraged about the amount of suffering in the world. I've realized that there are just some people we're not going to be able to help. It's hard to reach everybody.

At least now he was up-close. He had crossed the bridge.

It's difficult to piece together the first weeks of Jonathan's time in Africa. He began deleting his early blog posts after a few months, and then took down the site entirely. All that remains are the entries I happened to print out at the time. Our SMS messages tended toward the philosophical rather than the day-to-day. I guess I should have known when he began talking about helping child soldiers in East Africa that his time in West Africa was troubled. But I thought he was a restless twenty-year-old, trying to reach everybody.

The decision to go to Africa was not made lightly. We

could see it coming for nearly a year. We could see the stirrings in Jonathan's life, in his writing. In his first year of college, he wrote about his dream in a class assignment.

> I have a dream of complete self-abandon, of giving away all my things, of loving not myself but others. I have a dream that altruism is the ultimate form of freedom, for we are, more than anything, slaves to ourselves. I believe people are worth loving. I believe my heart can change, that it can focus outward instead of inward.

What I remember is his coming to me and his father shortly after starting his first semester of college to tell us he would commit to two years of filling up his mind if he could then spend a year emptying his heart.

> There is a great lack, I believe, in the way we see worth in others. Even our terminology is skewed. We use monetary metaphors like "value" and "worth" as though people are goods to be bought and sold. If we could look into someone else's eyes and understand how important they are, more than our possessions, more than our pride, more than our pleasure, then perhaps we would not just value them or find them to have worth but we would love them.

Later, when Jonathan's English professor wanted to nominate him for a writing award, the professor didn't take the usual route, which was to write a flattering essay on Jonathan's behalf and submit it to the awards committee. Instead he offered Jonathan's own words; in fact, these very words—about value and worth and love. Nothing was more compelling, according to the professor, than the conviction of Jonathan's own thoughts on paper. The professor read Jonathan's words aloud at the award ceremony just six days before Jonathan boarded the plane to live them out.

Before leaving for Africa, Jonathan looked back at the road that led him there:

> It has been my dream ever since I started college to travel the world and lend myself to a cause. I remember telling my parents one night a month or two into my first semester that I needed to get away and pour my heart into something other than a textbook for a while.
>
> God didn't allow me to travel the world right away, and the waiting period that followed resulted in seasons of depression and doubt. Looking back, I can see the lesson he was trying to teach me. Before I could go away, I first needed to learn to love the people around me. How was I going to serve the poor in another country if I wasn't serving the poor in my own backyard? He didn't want me to wait; I was supposed to be pouring out my heart right here at home. And I am still serving the poor in my own backyard. Only now, the backyard is about to get a whole lot bigger.

He followed his own line of reasoning, acted upon his intentions. He kept his promises. He finished two years of college. He gave away all his possessions. He loved the poor in his own backyard. He turned his heart outward. Then he signed on the dotted line and crossed the bridge to his dream.

We knew Jonathan would go eventually ("*GO!*" was

written in large letters on the chalkboard-painted wall of his bedroom, another visual reminder, like the quotes etched on his closet wall); we just didn't know when or where. There were some false starts and genuine obstacles, including the traffic accident in Richmond that cost him his Honduras fund. He had tried to go to Ecuador to work at an orphanage with some friends, but that plan fell through too. Jonathan said it was as if God had put a shock collar around his neck, and whenever he tried to leave the country, he would feel the sharp jab that kept him from straying beyond his own backyard.

Then one Sunday morning before church I began to pray for him. The kind of praying that starts out very noisy, then the words fail and trail off and you end up mostly listening. And what I heard was that my husband and I were to pray about whether Jonathan should take a year off school to serve overseas. Of course I didn't remember at the time that Jonathan had predicted this, had asked for it two years before when he started college. A lot had happened between then and now, including the false starts and missteps. At the moment it wasn't in Jonathan's plans; he was filling out applications to transfer to a new college in the fall. I told my husband right away what I had heard in prayer, asking him to hold the arguments against the gap year until we had more time to talk about it. I had the same concerns. Leaving college midway doesn't always end well. There was a real chance he wouldn't finish his education. And the timing on previous attempts to go had always been off.

A few minutes later Jonathan came down for breakfast, and he and Jeff were alone in the kitchen together. "Are you excited about starting a new college in the fall?" my husband asked. "No," Jonathan answered. "I really think I'm supposed to take a year off to serve instead."

As I was leaving the house for an earlier church service, I peeked in Jonathan's room and mentioned what I had told his father.

"After you heard us talking?" Jonathan asked.

"No, before."

Then the whirlwind began. Inquiries were made, and the first agency he asked accepted him. The money was raised in six weeks. Every detail fell into place. It was the first of many milestones, the first of many lessons. It was also the year we learned the cruelest of paradoxes, that a young man can be both called and led astray.

Yeast works its way through dough silently and invisibly; you don't know it's there until you see the dough rise, until the chemical reaction has already taken place. Yeast feeds on what's already there, consuming and changing it, reproducing itself, growing itself larger and larger by making empty spaces in the bread. In the heart. Jesus said to be on your guard against the yeast of the Pharisees. Because even a tiny amount can spoil good intentions, and ruin a calling.

The teaching of the Pharisees causes its own chemical reaction, converting freedom into bondage. It grows itself larger and larger until love is displaced by guilt. The yeast of the Pharisees creates an empty space so that motivation moves from the inside to the outside.

That is how legalism seeped into Jonathan's idealism. Slowly. Invisibly. Thoroughly. Just the slightest shift in direction, and he was following a broken compass.

That's what was happening inside of Jonathan. But there were also changes taking place around him, outside of him, in his new home in Africa.

I had written the good news in my journal:

We found out yesterday that the workers who are building the church in Cameroon are waiting for Jonathan to arrive (and even giving him a day to recover!) before laying the foundation stone. They want Jonathan to experience the beginning and the end, and everything in between—he will be there for the laying of the foundation stone and when the final nail is pounded into the roof.

We bought him steel-toed construction boots, purchased an anti-malaria medication that wouldn't cause his skin to burn during the long hours working in the sun. He was meticulously prepared.

Then it rained for three months. As it did every year at that time.

This evening we had dinner with the family who runs the Christian school. Unfortunately, they are severely understaffed. The responsibility of teaching every subject to every age group falls on just four teachers, but each one was smiling with excitement when I met them tonight. One man even expressed relief that he was not going to be the only male teacher anymore.

The founder of the school was eager to discuss ways I could contribute. Along with the planned guitar lessons, we explored other possibilities such as reading, writing, and communications classes.

Then school let out for the summer.

Jonathan had just arrived in Africa, but construction on the church and the bakery was suspended because of the rain. It turned out the foundation stone on the church was never laid, with or without Jonathan. The guitar lessons were put on hold, because school let out for the summer. As it did every year at that time.

He was up-close, but his hands were tied. Or empty. No guitar, no hammer. A familiar despair began to set in. But then he remembered. He had been promised that he would be free to pursue his interests and follow the Lord wherever he may lead.

That Sunday morning after I prayed for Jonathan I went to church and during the song service an image began to form in my mind. It was the smooth silk casing of a cocoon.

"God said the cocoon was Jonathan," I wrote in my journal later that day, "was the time of isolation and gestation he has experienced since his return from Honduras. It is the reason he wasn't able to go before, the reason for the shock collar. But now it's time for Jonathan to emerge from the cocoon, and that struggle to emerge will make him into the man that God intends him to be."

What takes place inside a cocoon is a change that happens slowly, and invisibly too. The caterpillar digests itself from the inside out. Its body is broken down and rebuilt—into something new. The process is internal; nothing invades and overtakes as yeast does, but what is new is created from what is already there.

It's not a chemical reaction. It's a transformation.

Before Jonathan left for Africa, he received an e-mail from a missionary doctor stationed in Cameroon; someone had sent her a link to the article about Jonathan's trip that ran in our local newspaper. She and her husband operated a hospital in the city where Jonathan would be living; in fact, the hospital shared a wall with the medical clinic where he would be serving. This was surely more than coincidence; even more surprising were her shared experiences with Jonathan: she was homeschooled, she grew up in Virginia, she went to college in our hometown. It gave us immediate peace and further assurance to know someone would be waiting on the other side of the Atlantic with a complete understanding of Jonathan's background—as an American, as a Virginian, as a missionary. Even their educational backgrounds were the same. She and her husband would be there to help absorb the culture shock, to ease his transition into

African culture. Jonathan's needs were being met before his feet even touched the red clay soil.

Once Jonathan realized his main reasons for coming to Africa were on hold, the ones he outlined in his support letter, the ones promoted by the newspaper, he tried to find other things to do with his time, to fill the hands that were emptied just after he arrived. He didn't cross the seas to sit alone in a soggy bedroom. And running a busy hospital requires many hands. Dr. F and her husband would welcome his help, his friendship.

Jonathan believed what he read in missionary books and saw in documentaries, that the hearts of African people were simple, noble, and pure. Africa, once called the Dark Continent, was now the last bastion of light, maybe the last sacred place on earth. Stories abound and are quickly disseminated about African children sharing freely; in one popular story they refuse to compete for a single basket of fruit, but hold hands and run toward the coveted prize set before them by an anthropologist. Beautiful and barely dressed, they are the antidote to Western greed. Tired of American materialism, Jonathan hoped not only to live among the poor but to learn from them. To see firsthand those who didn't use monetary metaphors like "value" or "worth." To live with people who cherish others more than possessions (which must be easier to do when you don't have many). To experience those with the innate ability to look into someone else's eyes and understand how important they are.

If he had a selfish goal, it was this. If he had a selfless goal, it was also this. He sought the purest form of Christianity. He sought the purest service to God. No longer bound by material possessions, he could live out his dream of complete self-abandon.

On his third day in Cameroon, Jonathan experienced his first African church service, the one he said would "ruin you to anything else." And if he had stayed in Africa for two weeks, the length of his previous mission trips, he would have that image in mind still. But he wasn't in and out over spring break, with souvenirs and snapshots and sad stories.

We had been told by Peter in one of our family meetings with him prior to Africa that the greatest spiritual need among his native Cameroonians was biblical training. We understood this to mean lack of resources as well as dearth of seminary training. Jeff has a seminary education, and realizing its importance, we raised extra funds to send pastors from all over Cameroon to a school of ministry. At the time we didn't know what supplied the wellspring of the country's theology. It flowed mostly through the airwaves, a shiny blend of Pentecostalism and prosperity gospel shipped over from the West Coast of the United States. "Signs and wonders and money" is how one mission guide recently described the church culture in Cameroon. During another church service Jonathan attended, the pastor turned the word "testimony" into "taste of money." He insisted that part of each believer's testimony—his or her personal story of faith in God—should include a taste of money. He declared it over the people, waving his handkerchief as they jumped and cheered. He prayed that each unmarried woman in the church would find a "handsome" man, a man with "some" money in his "hand." More jumping. More cheering. His sermon was filled with monetary metaphors of worth and value, as if faith in God were a good to be bought and sold.

At first Jonathan thought it was just bad timing. Whenever he tried to meet with Dr. F and her husband, to attend their home Bible study or volunteer in their hospital, an errand would arise that required his attention, even if it were just to ride along in the car with the local mission director. Peter had flown back to the United States after settling Jonathan in the home of the local director, Mosi, a young West African man who had just taken a wife. Finally Jonathan confronted him about the timing and found out the truth: Jonathan would never be permitted to befriend or work with them, because Dr. F and her husband were the wrong kind of Christians.

Jonathan had already discovered, when he tried to join an outreach that wasn't hindered by rain or the school calendar, that he was not permitted to work with non-Christian organizations. He had canvassed some villages with a few locals who were trying to educate other Cameroonians about services for disabled children. He was chastised when he returned to his African home for helping nonbelievers with their cause.

But now he was being told that other Christians were off-limits too, if they were the wrong kind. When Jonathan asked what was wrong with the doctor and her husband's beliefs (that were in a well-established denomination with missionary hospitals all over the globe), he never received a satisfactory answer. Finally he contacted Peter directly. We talked about their conversation via SMS, short text messages sent via Skype.

AMY: Did you hear back from him?

JONATHAN: Yes

JONATHAN: Basically he doesn't really want me to see Dr. F anymore

JONATHAN: Or associate with anyone he has not met yet

JONATHAN: So no more hanging out with them, the Peace Corps volunteers, other Cameroonians, etc.

JONATHAN: Unless it's strictly his organization

JONATHAN: Because it reflects badly on the organization

JONATHAN: He does not want me going to church or attending Bible study with Dr. F

JONATHAN: He won't let me crash at their house

JONATHAN: So for the next year I am prohibited from

hanging out with anyone other than the small group of people associated with his organization

JONATHAN: We can Skype now, but I'll have limited communication

AMY: Okay

JONATHAN: I'll be reduced to mhhm's and no's

Since Jonathan lived with the ministry director, he could only answer yes and no questions—and not make any comments—when we talked via video. His Internet access had been set up in the young couple's common living area, and they were there whenever he tried to contact us. That's why we often resorted to typing messages back and forth.

Through further talks with Peter and Mosi, it became clear who the "wrong kind of Christian" was: anyone who wasn't either servicing or financing the small mission agency.

So most days Jonathan sat alone in his soggy bedroom, put on the shelf like a trophy for show, while the rain came down and the schoolhouse sat empty and the hospital made do without his help. A young American had come to Africa, bringing lots of money with him, and that seemed to be enough for now. He wasn't permitted to follow God wherever he may lead. "If it were up to me, I'll be spending quite a bit of my time here," he said of the village that captured his heart. But it wasn't up to him. He had never really left his cloister closet. Or his cocoon.

CHAPTER 8

THE AFRICAN WAY

. . . So to add to the isolation I already feel, they are taking away the only bright parts of my stay here, the only place I feel encouraged and refreshed and peaceful.

—SMS message from Jonathan, week six in West Africa

JONATHAN COULD HAVE TAUGHT GUITAR lessons to the children at the orphanage, since their school and home are in the same place. But the crate of thirty guitars he had gathered up from generous donors before he left the United States was being held up in customs, even though they were shipped before he was. They arrived in Cameroon nearly four months after he did.

He also discovered that the suspension of the building projects had less to do with the abundance of rain and more to do with the dearth of building supplies. Either the supplies had yet to arrive or yet to be ordered, he wasn't sure which. The image of the workers staying their hammers until Jonathan landed was, to use a builder's term, a façade.

There was an occasional outreach, and he did set up digital record-keeping for the medical clinic, although he was convinced no one would keep it up once he was gone. Mostly what they wanted him to do was draw crowds as a white-man evangelist. "They want me on stage as an evangelist when in my heart I'm the guy walking through the crowd just letting people know they are loved," Jonathan told us at the time.

It's not that he had a problem with evangelism, even though the main purpose of his trip had always been service-related. But the gospel being preached by his mission agency had not escaped the current shift in Christian culture in West Africa. It, too, was about signs and wonders and money. It, too, took its cues from the health-and-wealth gospel flashing on the TV screen, a daily message of blessing from their favorite American preachers.

Pennsylvania State University professor Philip Jenkins documented the explosive growth of the prosperity gospel in West Africa, especially Cameroon's neighboring Nigeria: "The main growth businesses are gangs and evangelical churches which promise a better life."[1]

Who better to offer that life than a young American, fresh-faced from the land of opportunity? "Americans can preach the gospel in their churches," Mosi told Jonathan, "because you have all your needs met." But there was no such luxury in West Africa. In Cameroon's churches you have to promise things.

Jonathan preached when he was asked to, felt his heart sinking, felt his conscience burning. He tried to resist, but he was being initiated into another folkway of the African culture, with roots that ran deeper than the false gospel of the day. The centuries-old tradition was called "The African Way," and there was only one tenet: you do it because I said so.

The household code in Africa, we were later told by a veteran missionary, is very simple. The man is the sole monarch; his rule is absolute. If you are his wife, if you are his child, if you are a visitor in his home, he has complete control over you. No matter if the visitor is an adult; if he is younger than you, he is treated as your child. Worse still, if he is also in some ways your employee or volunteer, then servanthood becomes servitude. Once Jonathan became aware of this—once he saw it applied to himself, Mosi's new wife, and the other young Africans who volunteered for the organization—he confronted Peter about it. "Yes, it's true," he said. "You should see how pastors treat their wives in Cameroon. That's what I was like. That's what I would still be like, if I hadn't come to the States. It took seeing others and how they treated and led others differently for me to change." And then he added, "Feel free to take Mosi aside and teach him from the Scriptures that his behavior is wrong." But that is not the African Way.

It was late Sunday morning when the note popped up on my computer screen:

very sick. please pray.

It was hours before we were able to contact Jonathan to find out what was wrong. He had been up all night with a host of symptoms: vomiting, diarrhea, a fever, a sore throat, coughing. He was unable to eat or sleep, and most alarming, his throat was closing up. He called Dr. F, who suspected malaria and asked that he be taken to the hospital right away. Instead, Mosi pulled him from bed to attend an hours-long church service. Jonathan sat on the bench, cradling his head in his arms, and he was pulled to his feet, jabbed in the ribs until his hands were raised in worship, the African way.

Once he had seen a doctor, Jonathan called to tell us he did not have malaria, but his illness was in fact mosquito-related. He would recover after a few days of medication and rest. Mosi was with Jonathan when he called, was on the line with him when he called, so we didn't know for many weeks that he had been forced from bed and made to attend church before being taken to the hospital. When Jonathan asked why he couldn't be taken directly to a doctor, Mosi said it would reflect badly on the organization if the missionary wasn't seen at church.

It wasn't because of our own expectations or desire for things to work out that we weren't putting the pieces together; it was because for a long time the pieces weren't making their way to us.

Jonathan's contact with Peter was not limited or surveilled, so he reached out to him for help. He put his concerns in writing, told him how he felt about the religious practices of the organization, about the preaching of "a gospel that is used as a mechanism to control others, that puts words in God's mouth, that teaches that Jesus came to make us all rich, that we're to claim all the material possessions we want." He told Peter that he had witnessed spiritual leaders proclaiming false prophecies over people and shoving them to the ground to cast demons out of them. Any attempt to resist was met with belittling or accusations of lying. The leader was always right, always in control.

And that's why Jonathan couldn't take Mosi aside and teach him from the Scriptures that his behavior was wrong. Instead of abandoning the African Way, the Christian men in Cameroon found, in their eyes, a religious justification for it. They gathered up the verses about headship and submission, about young and old, about slave and free, and baptized the ancient custom in Christianity, washing away its dirty cover with the Word of God. Their grip only tightened, now that it had the weight of the Almighty behind it.

"That is why Dr. F's place has become somewhat of a safe haven," Jonathan wrote to Peter, "the only place where I feel at peace, where I feel like the gospel is actually being preached without coercion or the endless rituals that turn Christianity into something completely unrecognizable.

"Endorsing this sort of religion is absolutely soul-crushing to me. I have never felt more trapped in my entire life. Especially when the last, small comfort of Dr. F and her husband has been taken away."

Peter responded that he agreed with Jonathan's assessment of the spiritual climate of his native Cameroon, encouraged him to try to work within the limitations, the idea that sometimes you have to do wrong in order to do right. He told Jonathan he would consider finding him a new place to live where he wasn't subjected to the African Way, that he would allow Jonathan to spend time with Dr. F and her husband so as not to starve out his spiritual life. This, Peter said, will be an experiment for both of us.

Jonathan's situation began to come into clearer focus. There were hints, vague messages, like one sent in the only real letter we received from him, just after Peter made his promises. "So many things have happened since I left. I feel like there's no way to have that full conversation until the ride home from the airport, you know? That conversation when it's all finished and you can look back at everything that's happened." He was alluding to his lack of privacy and Mosi's constant surveillance, but because his letter was so upbeat we never really caught on. He was trying to spare us the full story until it was all over and done with. We thought this was his high idealism flickering back, the hopefulness reignited. But the truth is we didn't have that conversation on the ride home from the airport. He was disoriented; he barely spoke.

That's because the new promises Peter made went the way of the building supplies and the guitars. They existed somewhere—crossing the ocean or held up in customs, perhaps—but they had no intention of reaching the Cameroonian shore anytime soon. If ever.

The pieces we finally started putting together were supplied by Jonathan himself, without his knowing it. It was the woodenness in his voice, the dramatic changes in his physical appearance. The ashen look. The sunken cheeks. The frequent illnesses, one that required him to be evacuated from a remote village during an evangelistic crusade. His writing voice became fainter on his blog, a ventriloquist dummy mouthing words. Then his laptop, his main source of communication, was destroyed when Mosi's small home flooded, and it was as if his last link to the outside world—to his past life—had been cut off.

Jonathan was determined not to let down his family,

his church, and his supporters; he vowed to soldier on. We knew he was being increasingly isolated, that there was a reason for the rapid deterioration in his physical condition. But he was never able to paint us a clear picture, to tell what was happening from his vantage point. And then one day, after another soul-crushing disappointment, he was able to say the words out loud. What was being done to him was not for the sake of his own protection, as we had been told, but to secure ownership. "I am not free," he finally admitted. "I am under house arrest."

Once we knew, as soon as we knew, we asked that Jonathan be sent home. We were told he could leave before the year was up, but only after certain conditions were met. His early release would have to be negotiated. He was required to do more publicity, to raise more money for the organization through his blog. They were squeezing out the last dollar, the last word, the last bit of show from the trophy on the shelf. We asked that Jonathan be sent home immediately.

The answer was no.

That's when we realized we had overlooked something significant. The buck didn't stop with Mosi. There was someone older than he was, someone above him in the hierarchy. Someone who had absolute rule. "That's what I was like," Peter had said. "That's what I would still be like, if I hadn't come to the States." But he had spoken too soon.

A few years in America had taught Peter to cover up. But Jonathan's refusal to do his bidding forced it out from behind the placid veneer. When he couldn't manipulate

Jonathan calmly, subtly, he reverted to the African Way. Do it because I said so, he now demanded. He threatened to declare Jonathan a liability, according to a waiver he signed, and demand he be removed immediately at his own expense if he didn't comply.

When Jonathan didn't give in to the threat, Peter withheld his plane ticket from him. The one Jonathan purchased with the money he raised. Peter held it hostage. Held him hostage.

In the end, the bridge he offered Jonathan to reach his dreams only provided a way there. It was rigged, triggered to explode. It would collapse beneath his feet.

In 1971, twenty-four healthy male college students who were the same age as Jonathan volunteered for house arrest. It was technically basement arrest: they were isolated in the basement of Stanford University's psychology building as part of a two-week experiment funded by the Navy. The study was designed to induce disorientation and depersonalization in the participants by making them feel like prisoners.

In the footage of the study, Philip Zimbardo, the psychology professor conducting the experiment, gives instructions to half of the students, those who are assigned the role of prison guard:

> You can create in the prisoners feelings of boredom, a sense of fear to some degree, you can create a notion of arbitrariness that their life is totally controlled by us,

and they'll have no privacy. We're going to take away their individuality in various ways. In general, what all this leads to is a sense of powerlessness. That is, in this situation we'll have all the power, and they'll have none.[2]

After only thirty-six hours, one of the college students assuming the role of a prisoner began to show signs of extreme stress. But, Zimbardo noted, "It took quite a while before we became convinced that he was really suffering and that we had to release him."[3] Over the next few days, half of the "prisoners" had to be released early due to severe psychological distress.

The experiment was abruptly stopped after only six days because of the rapid deterioration of the participants who had been isolated and watched and controlled. And because of the increased abusiveness of the students who had been assigned absolute rule. (While half of the "prisoners" had to be released early, none of the "guards" left.) The experiment was halted only when an outsider, overcome by the dramatic changes in the participants, questioned the morality of what was being done. From boredom to fear to no privacy to no power. A group of young healthy college males had been stripped of their identity, made powerless, in less than a week.

"I began to feel as if my past has been wiped out," Jonathan told us. "As if the first twenty years of my life never existed. As if I had no history, no family, no friends. Nothing in my life happened before I stepped foot in West Africa."

The Stanford experiment concluded that it was the

situation and not the personalities of the participants that resulted in the abuse and distress. Not every social scientist agreed with the findings, so it was replicated, in one case with Christian kids from good homes and with strong spiritual backgrounds. When Wheaton College took on Zimbardo's experiment, they did so anticipating different results. Not only did they get the same results, but some of the most significant changes in the students took place after only an hour. The situation of abuse and control always turned out the same: the reins of the one in control ever tighten, while the powerless one acquiesces, turns ever inward.

Jonathan called him "Papa."

"Papa" is a term of endearment in West Africa, one that grants a spiritual leader special status as father. Jonathan called Peter "Papa" and meant it; he was a surrogate father in a strange land to take the place of his father back home. Peter was only physically in Africa with Jonathan at the beginning of his trip, but this was Peter's home, his people. He was Jonathan's primary lifeline to the outside world. A father is important especially when you feel disconnected from your past, as if you never had a family to begin with.

Do it because I said so, Peter demanded at the end. Do it because God said so, Papa had been insisting all along. Too late we had the final piece, the reason Jonathan had kept us in the dark, the reason he had stayed so long. More than anything else, Jonathan wanted to do what God said. He already knew that serious servants of God were tested. They were called upon to give more, endure more. This was the call he didn't want to miss; this was the test he didn't want to fail.

The African Way had been a last-ditch effort, a showing of the hand Peter had been keeping close to his chest from the beginning. He had found Jonathan's tender spot. And that, more than the overt demands and perpetual surveillance, more than the captive plane ticket, had allowed him to hold our son hostage from across an ocean.

Desperate to get Jonathan out of Africa, we considered every possibility: Do we get the State Department involved? Do we fly to Cameroon ourselves? A church offered to buy Jonathan a new ticket. A pastor friend offered to fly over and retrieve him under the cover of night. Finally Jonathan's church, where he served as youth leader, stepped in and secured his release home.

The ticket was returned to Jonathan on his twenty-first birthday. But there was no celebration, just the ending of what Peter called "an experiment for both of us." Jonathan's psychological distress, the stripping away of his power and identity, didn't last for six days but for four-and-a-half months. It didn't take place in the basement of a college classroom building surrounded by familiar faces, but alone in a small room in a strange country. It wasn't an experiment with controls and guidelines and outside observers. It was real life. His real life. And it was left in ruins. He gathered up the broken shards and packed them in a suitcase, leaving most of his personal belongings behind in Africa. His books, his guitar, the person he had been. Then the shadow of our son boarded the plane to come home.

CHAPTER 9

I'LL KNOW THE EXIT
WHEN I SEE IT

I AM HOME FROM AFRICA.

Every now and then I'll get a call from my host family, and we talk about the weather in Cameroon. I ask about their newborn son, the baby I didn't stay around long enough to see born. I ask if they received the package of American goodies I sent them.

They ask about my family, about how I'm doing, and I say I'm fine. But sometimes I don't answer their calls. Sometimes I'll go weeks ignoring their messages, staring at my phone until it stops ringing, until the call redirects to voice mail. My recorded inbox greeting used to say something about love, that I was glad the person had called, and whoever they were, I loved them very much.

Now an automated voice takes my calls.

It's strange to think how I drew inspiration and comfort from my cloister closet. How the walls chronicled my spiritual growth, how the framed photograph of the Honduran girl gave me the strength to keep going. How it ensured I would never forget her.

But now I wanted to forget.

The afternoon I arrived back in the States, I returned

to the place that symbolized the start of it all. I had failed my duty in Africa, but I could always return to my closet. I could always go back to the drawing board.

It's strange how a place that had kept my ideals so safe now felt so threatening, how a place that had occupied so much of my time could become so unfamiliar. The writings on the walls no longer inspired me. They taunted me. They reminded me that I had failed. I had failed the quotes; I had failed the Honduran girl; I had failed myself. But worst of all, I had failed the God of the universe: "Whatever you do for the least of these, you do for me." I managed a short nap, but then I rolled up my sleeping bag, untouched for what felt like a lifetime, belonging to a man I no longer recognized, and I closed the door like one closes a casket.

Over the course of the next year, I would return to the closet, not as a mourner paying respects, but as something closer to a grave robber. I painted over the walls; I took down and trashed the photograph.

Some reminders could be taken down, like the photograph. Others stare me in the face every day. Seeing the homeless on my way to work, running into youth I had mentored at the store.

Before Africa, I remember waking up one morning to the front page of the newspaper, a story about a stabbing in the downtown area. A young drug addict had hunted down his dealer after a botched transaction and stabbed him to death outside his house. I folded the page and looked at the mug shot of the suspect in question. I didn't have to see his name to recognize who he was.

He was just a kid, no older than I was, who had attended my church. A kid I had mentored during small group time at youth meetings. We lost touch, and I hadn't seen him at church in years. But I never thought the last time I would see him would be on the front page of a newspaper, right after he stabbed a man from behind and then through the heart. Right before a forty-year jail sentence.

Before Africa, I was driving down a main road, the same road that seemed to connect me to so many of the homeless in the area, when I saw a woman pacing back and forth in a small clearing off to the side of the road. It was Carmen.

I made a U-turn and pulled up next to her camp. She wore a thin, tattered dress, her arms stuffed with bundles of old newspapers and other recyclables. Her camp was littered with cardboard boxes, plastic tubs, and trash bags. Some bags held personal belongings, but most were full of trash. She was heading to Washington, DC, she told me. She was going to trade in her recyclables for cash once she got there. "Will you take me to the bus station?" she asked. I was scheduled to go into work soon, but I knew if she missed the bus she would be stranded. Together we loaded the back of my truck with everything she owned, and we set out on the southbound interstate.

Carmen was tired. Maybe it was the strain of packing; maybe she had been having trouble sleeping next to such a busy road. Her speech was confused; her thought patterns were hazy. Keep driving, she told me. I'll know the exit when I see it.

But we drove for miles, and Carmen never saw the exit.

In fact, she started dozing off. It was probably the truest rest she'd had in a long time.

We were almost an hour into our trip, and it was apparent Carmen didn't know where we were. I was going to be late for work, and Carmen, convinced she wouldn't make the bus in time, asked me to pull over so she could find a secluded spot to set up camp again. I dropped her off at the next exit and rushed to arrange her things in the woods before we attracted any attention. My stomach was in knots; she was displaced, in the middle of nowhere. I said good-bye to Carmen. I told her I was sorry. That was the last time I saw her.

I had helped Carmen countless times, but this is the only memory that comes to mind. I had helped the teens at my church countless times, but now I only think of one boy.

Because after Africa, it wasn't just myself I didn't recognize. I no longer saw the face of Jesus in the homeless; I only saw Carmen's face in the rearview mirror as I drove away. I no longer saw the face of Jesus in the youth, just the mug shot of the boy I failed to save. I no longer saw the face of Jesus in the Honduran girl, only the faces of the African children I left behind.

CHAPTER 10

IF ALL ELSE FAILS

I REMEMBER SEVERAL MONTHS AGO, SITTING IN THE grass in the wake of a car accident that resulted in my car getting towed, when a wave of hopelessness came over me. How do we change the world? How do we help people? What will happen to the people we don't reach? And then a verse popped into my head, and it was like God was giving me a promise: "Blessed are those who mourn, for they will be comforted."

That's the hope I have. If all else fails, I prayed, just let those who mourn be comforted.

We won't be able to reach everyone who needs our help on this earth, but God gives us the promise that he is still going to comfort them, and he's going to use you and me. That's why he put us here. We're here to love.

—Jonathan's blog post from Cameroon, explaining what led him there, one week after his arrival

Jonathan's grandmother is an old saint of a woman, the kind who wakes up in the middle of the night and prays for hours. She didn't want to distress us, but several times over the course of Jonathan's stay in Africa, she was woken up in

111

the middle of the night by her own sobs. She knew before we did. The pieces had made their way to her.

She had been especially supportive of Jonathan's trip, despite the risks, hustling up guitars and donations. While he was in Africa, she organized a garage sale for the orphanage bakery, which netted four thousand dollars in a single day. That brought our total offering to Peter's organization to just over twelve thousand dollars. It cost three thousand for Jonathan to live in Africa a full year, but he didn't make it that long, so much of the twelve-thousand was still in Peter's coffers when he came home. His grandmother's dream is to one day fly to West Africa, even at age seventy-nine, and eat bread made by the orphans in their own bakery. It's a pipe dream.

"Grandma says she loves you and she's not disappointed that you're coming home," I told Jonathan by phone a few days before he left Africa.

"Thanks. But I don't know if I believe it," he said.

"You don't believe she isn't disappointed?"

"No, the other thing."

"What do you mean?"

"I'm not sure I can trust her affection. It's been so long since I felt anything like that. I don't know how to explain it. I've been deprived of some things over the last few months . . ."

We never told Jonathan's grandmother that in Africa he had forgotten that she loved him.

The guitars finally arrived in Cameroon, just days before Jonathan's flight home. All thirty were to be kept at the mission's headquarters, to be used as the organization wished, Jonathan was told. The agency's volunteers could first pick through which ones they wanted, then the rest may be lent out to pastors and churches, or the agency itself might begin to offer guitar lessons. Jonathan resisted, made sure it was known that every person who donated did so with the assurance that the guitar would go to an African *child*. Many donors had made significant sacrifices; each instrument carried a story. An older man gave up the guitar he bought to earn his college music degree, another parted with a family heirloom from his Native American grandmother. A young musician who had been out of work and was newly employed handed over his entire first paycheck. A woman in grief used a portion of her father's inheritance to purchase $800 in guitar strings, anticipating the extreme heat would necessitate frequent replacement. Some of the donors asked that they receive a photo of the child who received their guitar, but not a single photo exists. The guitars belonged to him, Peter explained; his ownership extended to everything.

The orphanage begged us to send the four thousand dollars Jonathan's grandmother raised directly to them for the bakery, which was to be a joint project between the orphanage and Peter's organization. But checks had already been written and promises made. The orphanage had been the recipient of Peter's help before, when his agency built the orphans a modern, full-functioning kitchen, photos of which were shown during one of Jonathan's fundraising events. But when Jonathan got to Cameroon, he found the kitchen had never had adequate ventilation or the right equipment and it was turned into a meeting room. Meals for the orphans are cooked outside, over an open fire, near the farm animals. Still the before-and-after photos of the kitchen are shown, and money is raised.

Once we got a new computer to Jonathan, to replace the one lost in the flood, we were able to Skype again. The lapse in communication kept us a step behind, which is why we thought we were being forward-minded when we asked him one afternoon: "If you ever feel you are being asked to do something that violates your conscience, will you let us know?"

"My conscience?" It was more of a laugh than a question. He could speak freely because Mosi and his wife were away. "I parked that in the garage for the winter."

We didn't know until that moment that he felt that way, almost from the beginning, and long before the house arrest. It wasn't just the grandstanding or forced preaching or how he was mistreated; it's that he wasn't able to stop the mistreatment of other young members of the organization. It was witnessing how the organization conducted itself, did business, and not being able to intervene when promises were broken to the orphanage and the school and misrepresentations were made to the other Cameroonian ministries.

Having set aside his conscience, he began to take himself out of the equation more and more. I was familiar with this phenomenon, had studied it in graduate school, had taught it as a psychology professor at the university. In traumatic situations, people tend to separate themselves from their environments; it's a defense, a coping mechanism. A way to detach from painful thoughts and emotions. Sometimes children in abusive situations pretend they are someone or something else, like the clock on the wall. It also happens when a person feels depersonalized, as if his identity has been taken away, his past wiped out.

It's why his voice was wooden and his blog posts were disconnected. It's why his appetite left him and his ribs began to show through. It's why he didn't trust that his grandmother loved him. It's why we got Jonathan home but we didn't get him back.

His conscience was not the only casualty. He had parked himself in the garage for the winter.

When Jonathan's computer was destroyed in the flood, so was the database of his life: all his photos of family and friends; all his writings, journals, and college papers; videos he had taken; all his carefully selected music. The proof of his past was wiped out, a physical outworking of what was taking place inside. It not only offered physical evidence of what was happening to him, but it also delivered a new message. He felt as if God were saying, "You're not sacrificing fast enough. Now I'm just going to have to start taking stuff."

So Jonathan tried to sacrifice faster. He made one final desperate attempt to pass God's test. He fasted even though weakened by illness. He didn't sleep; he stayed up all night praying. He read a book on the Sermon on the Mount written by an African missionary who insisted Jesus's hard sayings were attainable if we just tried hard enough, believed enough; then the miraculous would be common-place. Jonathan confessed his sins: I'm not radical enough. I'm not really living the Sermon on the Mount. I will show God that I am serious, that he can trust me.

Jonathan was sure if he danced long enough and hard enough and chanted the right words, the rain would come down. God would appear. Without having slept or eaten, he launched out on his own into an African village searching for a sign that God had heard him.

Word spread among the villagers; a crowd gathered around the white-man missionary who said he was there to pray for their healing. There was much excitement, much expectation. Jonathan was being led around the village by a small teenage boy, who took him first to see his younger brother, whose right hip had been deformed since birth. Jonathan prayed fervently for the boy's healing, could feel the boy's pain surging through his own hip. Then he was handed a feverish baby. He prayed and prayed. He went from person to person, illness to illness.

But there was no healing, no rain. Still desperate, he asked if there was anything else he could pray for. That's when the teenage boy, his guide through the village, revealed that his father had died a few days before. He, his disabled brother, his distraught mother, now all alone. Jonathan began to pray and, overcome by emotion, started to cry, sobbing in grief for them. He prayed through his tears that they would be comforted. The two boys were taken aback by his emotion. Death was such a common occurrence in West Africa, a daily occurrence. Why was the white man crying over someone he didn't know? For a family he had just met?

Jonathan went back to his soggy bedroom with the sad knowledge that he had failed God. This was his last chance, and not a single person was healed. There would be no more rain dances. He had nothing left to sacrifice. This was the final soul-crushing disappointment. He could put up with any kind of abuse from Peter as long as he thought God would still use him, but now that he knew differently, he was ready to tell us the truth, to say the words out loud and come home.

He didn't remember what God had spoken to him when he sat in hopelessness in the grass after his car accident back home. He didn't remember what he had written in one of his first blog posts from Africa: "That's the hope I have. If all else fails, I prayed, just let those who mourn be comforted."

All else had failed. But had he?

Perhaps he wasn't in the village that night to represent the God who heals. Perhaps he was there to bring comfort from the God who grieves. To say *ashia*, we are together.

It was a singular relief when he finally walked through the side door designated for international flights. We couldn't go to him because of a barrier that kept waiting family and friends at a distance. We had to wait for him to come to us; the only thing for us to do was to take him in as he made his way across the room. His face was sallow and drawn, his shoulders arched forward, his chin came to a point. He was pushing a cart filled with a few belongings he could have easily carried by hand, but the cart was required by customs, for ease in inspection. I could almost see him as someone pushing a shopping cart along the main thoroughfare in our town, someone alone and neglected, living on the streets, like the people he loved so much. There was neglect about him, it overshadowed him; I could feel it in his ribs when I hugged him, welcomed him home.

As we left the airport he said, prayed, "Oh, God, please don't let me go back to doing the same old things I did before I left."

I reached back my hand. I'm not sure how the tradition started. When we're all traveling together in the car, I reach back my hand from the passenger seat up front, without turning around, and grasp at the air. Emily takes my hand first and holds it for a few moments. I squeeze tight and then release. Then I grasp at the air in Jonathan's direction, and he does the same. Sometimes I reach back with both hands, one for each of them. We adopted this routine when they were little and carried it all the way through their teen years. Usually it's during long trips when they are busy reading or listening to music; it's my way of saying, without interrupting, *Thinking about you, love you.* I reached back my hand to Jonathan. But he didn't take it.

He walked through the house, said how beautiful it was, as if it was the first time he had seen it. Customs had confiscated his butterfruit, a West African plum, but let him keep the plantain chips he had brought home for us. He pulled out a wicker basket from the cabinet and lined it with a paper towel, something we always did when serving snacks, a gesture so ordinary it seemed out of place. He paced the floor waiting for Emily to get home; she couldn't skip class to go to the airport because of a test. Then he slept deeply for a short time on the floor of his cloister closet, surrounded by his quotes, wrapped up in the bedding I never had the heart to remove.

The next morning I kissed him on the forehead while he slept, tasted the salt on his skin from a fitful night's sleep.

He woke up late in the day, and I made him a quesadilla for breakfast. He had requested quesadillas (his favorite birthday meal) for his homecoming dinner, but he had gone to bed early without eating much. He asked that we hold his birthday cake for another time. I spent the day washing the mold and mildew out of his clothes, everything stained a light shade of green, souvenirs of Cameroon's rainy season. He ate, took a real shower, laid in the flatbed of his truck to take in the sun. He spent the afternoon with a few of his closest friends.

Jonathan remembered the day I was praying for him in church and the image of a cocoon came to my mind. It was the day we knew he would be going away, and we all thought he would emerge from the cocoon in Africa. Instead, he felt more closed in, more constricted than ever.

"I did not come out of the cocoon by coming to Africa," he typed out in a SMS message one night a few weeks before returning home. "I'm being controlled here. This state was forced upon me. But I could have avoided it, if I had just done my homework."

He was right, of course, about still being in the cocoon. And he was right in saying his confined state was forced upon him. But he wasn't just held captive by Peter. Doing his homework may not have spared him. He would have to take a hard look at his own ideals. He could easily see the heavy burdens laid on the Cameroonians—a strict code of conduct, of dos and don'ts (mostly don'ts) that determined their spirituality. He saw the freedom on the farmer's face when he walked away knowing God loved him despite his lack of church attendance. But Jonathan couldn't see that he was also carrying a heavy burden. He couldn't see that the yeast of the Pharisees had also overtaken him. It wasn't just the self-denial. It was the relentless accusation that he wasn't doing enough. It was the drive to do good at all costs. It was the fear that he would miss God's call. It was the dread that he had failed God's test.

Coming home had only sprung him from his holding cell in Africa. He was home and safe but still bound.

Jonathan had left most of his things behind in Africa, but still felt heavy laden when he got home. He went through whatever he had left and gathered it up to take to Goodwill. One day I called upstairs for him but he didn't respond. His truck was still in the driveway so I climbed the attic stairs, and there he was, sitting on some carpet samples, his back facing me, in an area he and Emily had designated as their childhood clubhouse. (A demand for the password was written in permanent marker and childlike script on the beam above his head.) He was putting together his Hot Wheels track, which had lain in pieces on the floor for ten years. I climbed back down the stairs stifling a cry. The young man whose past had been wiped away reconnecting with the boy whose past had stood still, in the quiet corner of a clubhouse. I was sure he was reverting to simpler days. Jonathan insisted he was just finding more stuff to throw away. I still don't know which one of us is right.

What I do know is that the seeds of my son's destruction were sown while he was in Africa. What it took me longer to see was that the seeds of his healing were also sown while there. They would grow up together, like wheat and tares, until one would overtake the other.

CHAPTER 11

THE ONLY CERTAIN
HAPPINESS

AMY: Do you want to hear my dream or not?

JONATHAN: for sure, girl

AMY: The fire alarm goes off in the middle of the night in our house here. We all run out the front door, even Poppi. And then we see this tall figure's shadow in our little huddle. And it's you! You have slipped out the front door with us!

JONATHAN: haha

AMY: We can't believe it. Where did you come from? You say you arrived home from Africa two weeks ago . . . and you have been living in the attic. And then I remember all those times Poppi and I are downstairs with the house to ourselves and we hear what sounds like footsteps upstairs. We realize it was you all along—in the attic. But then I say to you: That can't be right! We just Skyped with you last night, and you showed us your room in Africa!

JONATHAN: it's a conspiracy

AMY: You say it's an illusion! You've recreated your Africa room in the attic to fool us!

JONATHAN: aww

AMY: For some reason you weren't sure how we would take your return, so you were hiding in the attic. But the fire alarm forced you out of hiding! We were *so* happy to see you! We couldn't believe you had been in the attic for two weeks or that you wouldn't have known how over-joyed we would be to see you.

JONATHAN: I probably would feel that way if I came back early

—SMS conversation with Jonathan in Africa

Two weeks after this conversation, Jonathan told us the truth about his confinement. That same day Jeff had said to him, "If a house is on fire, you don't have to pray about it, you just get out." Within a month he was home. In some ways he was still like a shadow hiding in the attic, unsure how his family—and his church and his supporters—would take his early return. But he had been forced out by the fire. He was trying his best to get his life back to normal. He had one more thing left to do, one more loose end to tie up. He would meet with the associate pastor who oversaw his ministry at the church, and then he could put Africa behind him, for good.

Jonathan had not returned to his church after Africa; no one in the congregation had even been told he had come home. I promised the associate pastor I would bake him a cake, or a dozen cakes, in gratitude for his part in getting Jonathan out of Africa. He was the one who helped release Jonathan's plane ticket. He contacted Jonathan after he returned and asked to meet with him one afternoon at the church. After their casual reunion, the associate pastor slipped out of the room and the senior pastor slipped in.

Jonathan was eight when he asked God, "Are you real?" When he returned from Honduras, he asked God, "Do you see?" They were questions prompted by childhood doubts, a teenager's crisis of faith. Now he would ask a third and final question of God. After this meeting. Because of this meeting.

Jonathan and I typed many messages back and forth during his final days in Cameroon. There wasn't much else for him to do. Peter wouldn't let him go to the school or the orphanage to say good-bye to the children. He wasn't permitted to tell the workers at either place that he was leaving. He was to pack up his things and sit tight until it was time for Mosi to drop him off at the airport.

During our exchanges, there were moments of confusion and moments of clarity. Jonathan remembers everything that happened before Africa and after Africa, but he has trouble recalling some of what happened while there, especially toward the end. It was difficult for him to process events, to find a place for them. They were like the data lost on his waterlogged laptop. But I wrote everything down in my journal, saved snippets of every conversation (every detail recorded as if I were a cop making an accident report). Some of the specifics of his day were lost on him, but an overall message seemed to be getting through.

JONATHAN: that's actually a huge thing i've learned here

JONATHAN: i'm done with the idea of changing the world, so to speak

JONATHAN: i just want to change my scope from here on out

JONATHAN: because doing good to your neighbor is something you can undertake in a small sphere

JONATHAN: i want to do good in a small sphere for a while

These breathless, one-sided conversations weren't unusual for Jonathan during his final days in Africa, or his first days home.

JONATHAN: i still want to do international work one day, but when i do, it will be to bring meaningful change in a small sphere

JONATHAN: neighbors are neighbors even if you live out in the middle of nowhere with only 2 or 3 of them

JONATHAN: if you think about it, you only need a few people to live the christian life

JONATHAN: you know?

AMY: Oh, absolutely. I'm just sitting here trying to take in what you're saying.

JONATHAN: like tolstoy's thing about living a secluded life in the woods with the opportunity of doing good to those who aren't accustomed to it

AMY: That's all Jesus called us to do, isn't it?

JONATHAN: i think i'm coming down from the attitude of trying to do it all

AMY: I think that's such an important thing to learn.

JONATHAN: i've never really been a numbers person

JONATHAN: that's why i enjoy one-on-one over the crowds

He was referring to a passage in Leo Tolstoy's novella *Family Happiness*:

He was right in saying that the only certain happiness in life is to live for others . . . I have lived through much, and now I think I have found what is needed for happiness.

> A quiet secluded life in the country, with the possibility
> of being useful to people to whom it is easy to do good,
> and who are not accustomed to have it done to them;
> then work which one hopes may be of some use; then
> rest, nature, books, music, love for one's neighbor—
> such is my idea of happiness.[1]

I typed up this passage and framed it and put it in
Jonathan's room before he returned home. It was a trib-
ute to his decision to do good to his neighbor in a small
sphere. He had a long way to go to recover, but it was a
beginning. He was making the first small cuts in the fiber
of his cocoon.

Jonathan had never intended to go to Africa under the
auspices of his church. Most of the literature he read took
a pioneer's approach to missions: do it bold, do it daring,
do it alone. But once the word got out and the newspaper
published his story and his campus picked it up and the
funds started coming in, his church decided to claim him
as its servant, as its son.

For shame to take hold, certain factors have to be in
place, and working together. There has to be an element
of secrecy, of not being able to verify the shaming. No
witnesses. When Peter chastened Jonathan, he did so via
Skype. He left no paper trail. He knew Jonathan's greatest
fear was being selfish; it was the disease that plagued his
generation, the self-centeredness he vowed to relinquish

the day he brought McDonald's to Bond across a busy highway. Peter knew this was Jonathan's greatest fear because he wrote about it in an early blog post from Africa, and Peter had to sanction every word:

> There is a self-centered beast in all of us. This beast, our pride, is the basis for every sin we commit. Think about it for a minute. Any act of violence, any lie, any disservice to our fellow man boils down to an act of selfishness, an outpouring of ego, of our pride. Pride is the voice telling us that we are more important than others. And that is why we sin.
>
> My eyes were opened when I understood this. Never before had I realized how selfish I truly am, and how destructive my selfishness is to others.
>
> Then it hit me—Jesus was the most humble person who ever lived. Now I had someone to look up to, someone who was the best example in history. Sure, I had always known Jesus was the Son of God, and that was reason enough to worship him. But I felt a new sort of awe, a new sort of admiration for him. I had a newfound love for him. Now that I understood the importance of humility, I had no choice but to follow Jesus.
>
> This decision, however, came at a dangerous price. It meant I had to start listening to the things Jesus said. These verses particularly spoke to me: "Sell what you have and give to the poor," "Take nothing for your journey," "Deny yourself and follow Me."
>
> Determined to take the words of Jesus seriously, I

embarked on a journey of self-denial. I gave away most of my possessions, I moved into my closet, and I slept on the floor. I was trying desperately to escape my consumerist American lifestyle. In many ways I gained much more than I lost. But it wasn't long before I started feeling empty again. Something was missing. Somehow, this minimalist lifestyle was threatening to make me just as self-centered as I was before. Though I was trying to deny myself, I was still focusing on "me." My actions were not yielding the opposite of pride; they were simply yielding less pride. I was learning that it is not enough to merely decrease selfishness. Jesus is asking for so much more than that.

There's a quote often attributed to Gandhi that says, "Live simply so that others may simply live." I like this idea. Perhaps that is the responsibility we must take on when we decide to stop living for ourselves.

All human beings are made in God's image; therefore all human beings have worth. Jesus understood that. After Jesus healed people, he just sent them on their way. And barely anyone even thanked him. Jesus was not only the most humble person who ever lived; he was also the most loving. Just as pride can be seen as the basis for all that is evil, love can be seen as the basis for all that is good. Why else would Jesus sum the law up into two commands, to love God and love people? Love takes care of everything. It covers all the bases. If you love God, you won't sin against him. If you love others, you won't sin against them either.

Jesus loved everyone. He accepted everyone. And he

THE ONLY CERTAIN HAPPINESS

did so without expecting anything in return. He didn't solicit donations, and he didn't make anyone sign a contract.

But Jonathan had signed a contract. If Peter couldn't legally keep Jonathan in Africa against his will, he could try a back door. You're *prideful*, Papa told him. You're *selfish*. Then Peter shut down his computer and went to bed, giving shame a chance to do its work.

Jonathan had not been told he would be meeting with the senior pastor. This was supposed to be a friendly catching up between two friends, colleagues. But once the switch was made—one pastor in, the other out—Jonathan was alone in the room with him. No witnesses.

Jonathan had served as a young leader in the church for several years. Before he left for Africa, the youth pastor acknowledged Jonathan shared the burden of ministry with him, especially by mentoring the teens no one else wanted to. The senior and associate pastors felt Jonathan was a natural leader and talked about his possibly planting a sister church one day.

The senior pastor opened their secret meeting by pulling out his Bible and reading a passage:

LORD, who may dwell in your sacred tent?
The one . . . who keeps an oath even when it hurts,
and does not change their mind.
(Psalm 15:1a, 4b)

Peter had shamed Jonathan by using his own words against him. More effective still was to use God's word against him.

Once Mosi knew Jonathan was leaving, he loosened his stranglehold. He wasn't supposed to. Peter had given him strict guidelines regarding Jonathan's final days in Cameroon, but Mosi didn't see the point. By the time word got back to Peter, there would be nothing he could do. Mosi let Jonathan roam free for a few days. He chose to spend time with Dr. F and her husband and another volunteer who was in West Africa with the Peace Corps. There were long conversations about faith and faithfulness that challenged his rigidity. He was just beginning to see the exacting nature of his own perspective, the legalism inherent in his radical attempts to save the world. The gate that allowed access to his brand of Christianity was narrower than the founder of the faith had made it. He knew now that he shouldn't have done it bold, daring, or alone. He began to experience what it might be like to be free. Not only free from his cell in Africa, but the mind-set that kept him in his cloister closet. The mind-set he admitted might have kept him hiding from his family in the attic, should he have to come home early.

The secrecy needed for shame to work isn't tied to a lack of witnesses only. You have to ensure the person being shamed never tells what was said or done in secret. The best way to do that is to make it personal. Start by calling into question his manhood, frame his return as an act of weakness. Then tell him his parents appear crazy, that their intervention in his rescue only escalated things. Tell him that "sin varies from culture to culture," so that the kind of abuse that's considered sinful in America may not be sinful in Africa. Tell him that unless there are bruises or evidence of adultery, you should stay where you are and keep your oath. If you don't feel you're making progress, you can come up out of your chair and physically intimidate the person you hope to shame, especially if your amplitude overshadows his frail frame. Then once the person's shoulders sag in compliance (that's the cue), you use your leverage to control what happens next. Because controlling what happens next is key.

The shame you've cultivated can't change anything; it can't reverse a decision. No one's getting back on a plane to Africa. But you can channel it into working on your behalf, and you can tell the young man that there is a prescribed list of people who can be told the truth—excluding the truth of this meeting, of course—about what happened to you. And that list includes your father and your mother and your sister. No one else may know. You are to tell non-list people that you had "philosophical differences" with your mission agency.

And then when the young man does, in fact, tell someone what you said, when he surprises you and tells his parents you think he's not a man and they are crazy, you invite his parents in for a meeting and, of course, you don't repeat anything you said to their son. But you go straight to the catch: no one may know what really happened. And if they and their son don't agree to silence, then neither do you—and you are free to say whatever you want about him from the pulpit. But that's not a threat. No, it's not a threat.

And perhaps the young missionary's parents, because he has already been so traumatized, encourage him to agree to the silence because they want it to be over and they don't want him hurt any more. And so you've won—and you didn't even need to come out of the chair this time—because of the fear and the pain and the shame. You sit back and you mark the young man off your to-do list, confident that he will never tell.

CHAPTER 12

STEPPING BACK

THE LAST TIME I MET with my mentor, an associate pastor who oversaw my work in the youth group and who supported my journey to Africa, we were jogging downtown and talking about the upcoming year. It was a familiar route, one we took almost weekly when I was a youth leader. It was the same road where I had seen Carmen pushing her cart, the same road where my friend had stabbed his drug dealer.

He asked how I felt being home again, if I was disappointed in God for how everything had turned out. I told him I was more disappointed in myself, that my expectations had been too high, that I had placed undue pressure on my success in Africa to determine my worth as a Christian. He asked what my plans were for the future, about where I wanted to go from here, and I told him I just wanted to take a break. A break from missions? he asked. A break from God, I answered.

I remember going up for prayer one night during a church event, several weeks before the arrangements for my trip to Africa had been finalized. I was looking for direction, some kind of confirmation from God that I was on the right path. I waited patiently while my mentor and an elderly woman prayed over another person in the congregation, and when it was my turn, I approached them and shared what was on my mind. As they began praying over me, my mentor said he felt like God wanted me to know that I was his beloved son, with whom he was well pleased. In minutes, we were both reduced to sobs. It was one of the only times I had witnessed a grown man cry like that.

But this meeting was different. He didn't assure me that God was pleased no matter what I chose. Instead, he said I was venturing into dangerous territory. I was going down a dark road, he warned, a road he'd seen many young people go down before me, a road that never ended well. He told me I shouldn't stop praying and reading the Bible, I shouldn't stop going to church. He told me I needed to come back to my congregation, to be healed by the very people who hurt me. He gave me a list of books to read and offered to meet with me on a regular basis in order to guide my healing process. Without God, without my church, I would become a lost cause.

His answer to my hurt was "more Jesus." But I didn't want more Jesus. At the time I didn't want more of anything. But that was the only avenue of healing I was permitted to explore. Otherwise, I didn't have his approval.

When spiritual growth is measured in intensity, the only direction you're permitted to go is off the deep end. To question your beliefs is to backslide, so you're told that the only way to get better is to dive headfirst into those existing beliefs with more manic zeal than before. But when you're never allowed to take a step back, to stop and ask yourself what you're doing and why you're doing it, you lose sight of what mattered to you in the first place.

My church was not interested in helping me foster my convictions, only in telling me what my convictions should be. Instead of asking, "What do you care about?" it was, "This is what you should care about." And that was the hardest part about post-Africa—differentiating personal conviction from obligation.

A friend once told me I was searching for the perfect soul-searching method. And in a way, what my mentor was offering that day was just another method to try on, just another formula to follow. But if I was ever going to figure out what I truly cared about, if I was ever going to separate what was important to me from what was important to God, to the church, to my mentors, I needed to stop relying on their cues. I needed to stop getting all my answers from them.

My church was not concerned with my well-being, during or after Africa. They were only doing what needed to be done to keep me among their numbers. The solution to every problem was always to stay in the group and not venture outside their protection. They were creating a dependency, positioning themselves as my only hope. It was as though they were saying, "You can't survive without us."

It was the same message the African organization had drilled into me from day one. And it was just as effective, for a time, in keeping me in Africa as it was in keeping me in church. I had left Africa, but I wasn't out of the woods yet. There was one last offer on the table, one last attempt to get me to stay.

You don't have to make a decision today, my mentor told me. Think about it for a week and get back to me when you're ready, he said. If I don't hear from you, I'll know which way you chose.

In the eyes of my mentor, I was choosing the path of least resistance. But for me, the hard thing to do, the right thing to do, was to leave. Once I saw how I was being used, how I was being shamed and controlled, I couldn't unsee. I couldn't carry on as though nothing was wrong. To do so would have been to dust off the blinders and strap them back on. It may have been easier to stay, but it would have been an absolute lie not to leave.

CHAPTER 13

THREE CHOICES

MY FAVORITE MOMENT WITH THE CHILDREN CAME ONE afternoon as we were singing songs with the guitar. One of the boys who happened to live in the area came over and set up a keyboard outside and started playing with us. Together we practiced the hymn, "The Steadfast Love of the Lord," and the two of us, along with some girls from the orphanage, performed it for the local church a few days later.

As I set out on what will surely be the longest and most challenging year of my life, I take comfort in the fact that his mercies will be there to meet me along the way, new every morning.

> The steadfast love of the Lord never ceases
> His mercies never come to an end

In the end, Jonathan was given three choices, which were spelled out in writing: (1) He could tell whomever he wanted what happened to him in Africa; (2) "We can agree to cover everybody with love with an agreed-upon statement and drop the issue." The agreed-upon statement was scripted by the church (by now he had experience as a ventriloquist dummy) and supplied words like "ministry differences" and "out of deference to love" and "I don't want to talk anymore"; or (3) He could tell "more of the story" to a "limited number of people" but he would have to submit a list of names to the church, so that they could call each person in for damage control. This option also required that Jonathan submit the following information, in writing: Who was spoken to? When did it occur? What was said?

If he chose Option 1, the pastor would be free to say, as promised, whatever he wanted about Jonathan from the pulpit to protect the church's reputation. If he chose Option 2, he would be lying, because it was untrue to say he left Africa because of philosophical differences. If he chose Option 3, he would be subjecting his friends (whether or not they attended the church) to needless scrutiny. His only real choice was to say nothing.

A few weeks after he agreed to silence, Jonathan was out one night with his best friends, two brothers, who had been preacher's kids like him. Until the church had financial difficulties, their father had been a pastor on staff at the church Jonathan attended. The three of them had always been close, but even more so after Africa. The brothers were the only two people Jonathan could trust, the only two he spent time with once he returned. That night they confided in him that after our family meeting with the senior pastor, he called their father aside, enlisted his help by asking him to sit each of his sons down separately and discredit Jonathan's story.

The church did no wrong, this man told his sons. Peter,

with whom the church intended to work on future missions, is a good man, their father insisted. It was all a big misunderstanding. And just like that, Jonathan's safe haven was ransacked, his last sanctuary defiled.

Everyone had agreed to stick to the scripted statement or to say nothing. Instead, the senior pastor had broken faith so that he could take the extra step to inoculate Jonathan's closest friends against the bad press. Jonathan had gone from poster boy to persona non grata. From fresh-faced leader to shamefaced outcast. And then, and only then, would he go from missionary to prodigal.

When Jonathan was asked to preach about his ministry to the homeless one Sunday morning at church, shortly after his return from Honduras, he was instructed not to talk about the hopelessness he felt when he saw the suffering of the Tolupan Indians. Those words were edited right out of his sermon. The pastor wanted to keep things upbeat and positive, which would have been difficult if Jonathan had told the truth about his experience. Now he was being edited again. Or scripted. His very words were supplied for him, and under the words, the message: what happened to you never really happened.

The church had done a simple cost-benefit analysis. We had been told that Peter's organization was only loosely associated with the church—that's how Jonathan found out about it—but when the church considered future projects, they came to the conclusion that Jonathan, no longer attending the church and no longer serving as youth leader (and yet, strangely, still under their authority), was out, but Peter's organization was still viable. As a bonus, Jonathan was the only living soul this side of the Atlantic who knew of Peter's reputation in his native Cameroon. Peter and his organization would continue to be in good standing as long as Jonathan kept quiet. "Cover everybody with love and drop the issue" translated into "cover up and drop the issue."

It would reflect badly on the church to be associated with scandal, or worse, failure. Silence would be best. Everyone shook hands and went home.

We didn't know then that other missionaries in the church had been called into similar meetings when they were mistreated by a mission organization or had to come home early. Had we known, we might not have felt so alone. Or singled out. For the "sake of the gospel," for the "unity of the Body of Christ," they too had been told to keep their mouths shut. No need to discourage future missionaries, or give current donors a reason not to give. They were asked the same questions Jonathan was asked: Are there bruises? Is there any evidence of adultery? And if the answer was no, no sin was committed. The missionaries should stay put or stay quiet. The questions seemed ill-fitting for Jonathan's situation, or any missionary's, but we learned the questions were the same gauge used to determine whether a woman was permitted by the church to leave an abusive spouse. Clear-cut questions are asked in this delicate situation, we were told, because it is often difficult to determine whether the woman is telling the truth. If she couldn't answer "yes" to one of these weeding-out questions, the senior pastor sent her back home. Using identical questions streamlined the process, kept the negative publicity to a minimum. No need to discourage future wives, or give current wives a reason not to stay. This same rationale applied when the associate pastor begged Jonathan to come back to the church, saying that Jonathan could only be restored in the crucible that burned him. The church had wounded him, and they would heal him. The message to missionaries and mistreated wives was the same: it is easier on us if you stay in your abusive situation.

"Why would someone who is so disappointed in God want to talk about him all the time?" Jeff asked me after another hours-long debate with Jonathan. The record was five hours. I opted out after three. I feel sure God opted out after four. But Jeff and Jonathan were still going at it.

The debates started soon after Jonathan returned from Africa and intensified after our meeting with the senior pastor. There were hard questions and strong anger from Jonathan's side. He had lost his church community and friends. He felt both his past and his future had been wiped out at the same time. The foundation of his faith, twenty years in the making, had been shattered. And his expectation that he would one day be an international worker lay withering in the African sun.

Sometimes they would start in the kitchen while we were making dinner. A question was asked, and a long theological debate would follow about whether Scripture is inerrant or infallible, who goes to heaven, and if there is a hell. If, as a curious eight-year-old, Jonathan had asked questions about general versus special revelation and how the Godhead could be three in one, his questions as a disillusioned twenty-one-year-old were even more penetrating. But it was all smoke and mirrors, a way to distract those around him from the real source of his pain.

One night Jeff and I climbed into bed, exhausted from another heated argument. But Jonathan wasn't finished. He followed us upstairs, stood at door of our darkened bedroom, his arms outstretched against the frame. No more arguing over salvation or interpreting Scripture or the basics of sanctification. Instead he asked his third and final question of God.

"How long do I grovel at his feet?" he cried. "He's not there."

Jonathan was unable to go back to college because he was having problems concentrating. A voracious reader, he could now only focus for a few minutes at a time. We didn't know for months that his inability to concentrate was a sign of depression.

We had missed other signs too. His anger, irritability, social isolation. The heavy drinking, something he never did before Africa. His risky behavior. All signs of depression in men, who tend to act out, lash out when overwhelmed by sadness. "If you expect me to curl up in the fetal position," he said his first full day home, "you're going to be disappointed." All his pain was pushed outward.

He didn't seem to trust us anymore. He brought that distrust home with him from Africa, packed it up in one of his empty suitcases, and it was only reinforced when his church turned its back on him. "I'm sorry," he texted one day after another fight. "I think I must have some complex that everyone is out to get me. Even you and Dad. Even God."

That's why, recalling his experience with God at age eight, I thought he was being rebellious when he asked me if God was real. I thought he was trying to hurt me. But Jonathan wasn't the only one rewriting his life story or reinterpreting his childhood memories. We were both wrong about his first encounter with God. I remembered it as rebellion because I was looking through the same filter Jonathan was; we were both changed after Africa. Not then and not now was it rebellion in any real sense. The same little boy who wanted to know the reality of God was the same young man who could no longer feel his presence. He was asking again—through his depression, through his distrust, through his anger: how do we know God is real?

You shouldn't be afraid to ask God to show you he's real, I had told him then.

The diagnosis was *major depressive disorder, single episode, severe*. He began taking medication, but that's not the reason we were on our way to the lab for blood tests that day, when he reached across the front seat of his truck to take my hand. The day he said he thought God hated him.

151

Initial blood tests after the depression diagnosis had shown elevated liver enzymes. The doctor had to rule out certain things, due to his exposure overseas and his behavior once home. Jonathan walked up to the window at the lab, handed the receptionist his doctor's order requesting tests for Hepatitis B and C and HIV. I sat in the waiting room while blood was drawn. Last spring I sat and waited while he got his vaccinations for Africa. "How is this possible?" I would have whispered under my breath if I had been able.

Jonathan had written in an early blog post from Africa that he was not afraid of something that could hurt his body; he feared only what could hurt his soul. But his hurt soul was now wreaking havoc on his body. Self-denial and self-abuse are at opposite ends of the same continuum. Jonathan admitted that he wasn't just trying to numb the pain, the pain of the abuse in Africa, the betrayal once home. He was trying to feel compassion again, to jar awake the instinctive sense he had since he was a little boy. That sense had matured as he grew older into a love for the homeless, a love for a struggling friend, a love for a tribe of Indians. But his recent experiences had nearly killed that part of him. It was like a body coding on a cold surgical table; he tried desperately to jolt it awake.

"Do you still think God wanted me to choose that option?" Jonathan texted me one night when he was out drinking. We were the ones who encouraged him to choose silence. We had wanted to protect him, but we only made matters worse. Placing conditions upon his truth-telling, refusing to let him tell his story, had struck the death blow to his faith.

As the evening progressed, more questions came. "In all honesty," he texted, "are you guys afraid for my salvation?" When I said I wasn't, he asked, "Then why did I see you crying?

"The only explanation I have is that you and Dad are afraid I'll be burning in hell for all eternity.

"And if God is love . . . hopefully, it's not that tenuous."

Jonathan agreed to follow the church's sanctions, and Peter agreed to submit a report to the church with an explanation of how the remaining funds in Jonathan's account would be spent. Instead, Peter turned in a spreadsheet that accounted for every penny Jonathan had raised. His eight thousand dollars was enough to pay for his expenses in West Africa for over a year and a half, but by Peter's accounting, every dollar had been spent in just over four months. The expenses were documented in West African CFA francs, not American dollars, making it difficult to follow, but what was clear was a grand total at the end showing all of Jonathan's money was gone—and, therefore, Peter was no longer accountable to the church for its use. With the help of an exchange calculator we discovered that $1,400 from Jonathan's donations was used for shipping the organization's supplies, which had been kept in storage in the United States, across the ocean. Of course, the guitars were in that crate, but they only accounted for a small percentage of the full load. Jonathan was not informed that his donors would be paying for the organization's hefty transport fees, nor was he even asked.

He was also charged rent for ten months, even though his room sat empty for six of those months. Fuel for the organization's trips taken during Jonathan's time in Cameroon was paid for from his account. The rest of the money was nickel-and-dimed in an endless list of insignificant entries: repair to the cot Jonathan slept in, transport of the cot once repaired, tablecloth, snack at airport, the list went on.

The donations from faithful friends and family had been misused, and none of it could be returned. Still, Jonathan kept quiet. Covered over, issue dropped.

All the blood tests came back negative. There was relief but also a new wave of concern at how much he had changed, at how his behavior had made him susceptible to illness and injury that would have been unthinkable just months before. It was the first time since he came home that he had a physical marker of the spiritual damage caused by Africa and its aftermath. True to his word, he had not curled up in the fetal position. Not on the outside.

But the abuse he had endured began to seep from spirit to body. And his own sense of failure, firmly established by the religious leaders around him, caused an internal self-flagellation that slowly crippled him outwardly. The spirit and body were not separate, as he had thought. He couldn't neglect one and expect the other to flourish. He couldn't choose only one to be concerned about, in Africa or anywhere. If Jonathan was going to get better, he would have to confront both—the harmed body and the harmed soul.

I confess that for many months I prayed that the son

who left for Africa would resurface in the son who returned from Africa. One day I was messaging a friend online and trying to sum up the last few months in the best way I could. I typed the words I couldn't say out loud: the kid who left is not the same kid who came back. A few minutes later Jonathan came downstairs to make coffee. I walked into the kitchen, and he put his arms around me. After a long hug, he said, "I'm the same kid, Momsies. Just in far worse circumstances than when I left." He had been upstairs when I was typing the message online. There was no way for him to know I had just used the exact same words, no way for him to know that he was refuting my claim.

Unless there was a part of him that was still connected, still trusting. A part of him that wasn't coding on a cold surgical table. A part of him that had made it home.

CHAPTER 14

RUNAWAY

Denial: There's nothing under the bed.
Distance: There's a monster under there.
Self-discovery: The monster reflects
something inside me.

—PETER ROLLINS, PHILOSOPHER AND THEOLOGIAN

THE MONSTER UNDER MY BED, or rather, the monster in my cloister closet, was legalism. It was the same monster I saw in the Cameroonians, in the mission organization, in my church. It was a monster I failed to see in myself. It was a monster I thought I'd left behind.

But isn't it curious how the things we hate about others are often the very things we hate about ourselves? The monster I was fleeing had been with me all along. And just as running from my problems had led me to Africa, running from my problems had now led me back home. The old adage had proven true: wherever you go, there you are.

I was a spiritual runaway, always fleeing the scene, always hopping from one spiritual bandwagon to the next. But after all this coming and going, after years spent in denial and chasing dead ends, I was ready to admit that my problems were not solely external, that I had been carrying baggage too. I was ready to unpack the monster, to finally acknowledge it was there, and to call it what it was.

The legalism I rejected proclaimed, *Look how good I am because of what I don't do*. The legalism I accepted proclaimed, *Look how good I am because of what I do*. But the latter is just as shallow as the former. Both are self-serving. Both say, *Look at me.*

While the old legalism took its cues from Old Testament commandments to abstain, the new legalism takes its cues from Jesus's commands to act. It wasn't difficult for the Pharisees to press legalism into the law, but modern-day Pharisees have done something more difficult. By sneaking legalism into a freeing gospel, they've turned Jesus into a Pharisee too. This Jesus was sent to fulfill the old requirements, only to turn around and give us new ones.

At the core of legalism is the belief that devotion to God can be measured. Number of souls won, hours spent in prayer, number of days fasted, dollars given to charity. It becomes a way to prove to yourself, to your peers, and to your God that you're actually taking Jesus's words seriously. You're not the average Christian: you're radical.

Just as the Pharisees made a contest of following the law, the new Pharisees make a contest of good deeds and sacrifice. They are intent on "getting back to what Jesus really said." And while these buzzy phrases sound nice, the application is less about gaining a deeper understanding of Jesus and more about taking Jesus's words and running with them. For these radical Christians, anything less than a literal application of the Bible is to take the easy way out, an excuse for lazy Christians who don't have the discipline to obey the hard sayings of Jesus.

This is why zealous young Christians are instructed to give their lives over to God and go wherever he leads, no matter what the cost. Sure there will be danger. Sure you might find yourself in peril. But this is what God wants of you; he'll work out the details. All you have to do is pick a spot on the map, hop on the plane, and go.

But who else was told to put himself in harm's way and let God do the rest? Wasn't Jesus offered the same temptation by Satan in the wilderness? "Throw yourself down from the highest point of the temple," Satan challenged. "If you are who you say you are, God won't let you fall" (Matthew 4:5–6, paraphrased). It was an opportunity for Jesus to prove his special proximity to God, a chance to demonstrate a show-stopping act of faith.

But manufactured hardship is always for show. Radicals forsake big houses and nice cars for mud huts and orphans. But to wear sacrifice as a badge is to trade material status symbols for spiritual ones. It is baptizing attention-seeking behavior, confusing "making an impact" with "making a scene."

The same kind of exhibitionism Jesus refused to take part in is now the very thing radicals think Jesus expects of them. As the contest escalates, the question becomes, How much trouble can I land myself in? How can I get myself thrown in jail like the apostles? How can I get myself killed like the martyrs?

Before long, merely doing good is not good enough. You have to do the most good. Even Jesus's command to love your neighbor falls short if the new standard is to do as much good as you can, to as many people as you can, as often as you can. And since no one can fulfill these unrealistic expectations, no one is satisfied, no matter how much they do. And this creates a perpetual cycle of low self-esteem, inadequacy, and discontent.

I wasn't doing enough good, which meant I wasn't good enough.

And though I never would have said so at the time, I secretly felt that God wasn't doing enough good either. How long must I pray and fast so that God would do his job? How long do I have to pick up his slack and keep him accountable? I thought that through my vigilance I was giving God a hand, doing him a solid, helping him out.

When I left Africa, not only did I have to admit that I had gotten myself into a terrible situation, but I had to concede that I was not radical enough. I could no longer follow the new rules. I could no longer live up to the new standards. In the end the gate had become so narrow that I couldn't squeeze through.

I didn't leave legalism. Legalism shut me out.

CHAPTER 15

RESULTS NOT TYPICAL

Not all those who wander are lost.

—J. R. R. TOLKIEN'S WORDS, NEWLY
TATTOOED ON JONATHAN'S UPPER ARM

IT WAS MID-DECEMBER, MIDDAY, AND I had been think-ing and praying when the idea struck me. I ran upstairs to Jonathan, who was still asleep, had slept through most mornings for the three months he had been home. "Let's write a book together," I said. "Let's tell your story." He turned over, mumbled, "Okay." Later he wondered if he had dreamed it.

It's risky to begin a project without knowing how it ends. We didn't have any idea how or when Jonathan's story would resolve itself, if ever. We were writing through the pain, not neatly afterward, and it was messy and uncomfortable and there were days I wished I had never said the words out loud. During one writing session Jonathan accused me of wanting to write the book to "heal" him, as if healing were the worst desire a parent could harbor for her child. We argued a lot. After one particularly virulent fight, I walked across the hallway from Jonathan's room, where we had been working, and glared at my husband, who had heard every word: "Still jealous I'm writing a book with our son?"

Jonathan and I talked through everything that hap-pened. We wrote everything down. I've spent the past two days combing through the fruit of that labor, 293 pages of typewritten notes. It's a chronicle of all the thoughts and words and ideas exchanged between us over the last year. There are conversations and text messages and phone calls and long, breathless oracles. Every page shows how one thought led to another, how each belief was deconstructed and remade, like a cocooned caterpillar digesting itself in order to build itself anew. But more than a chronicle it is a map: you can get there from here. But first you have to do the work—the painful, rip-your-guts-out work—of telling your story.

It is unusual to have a day-by-day account of how someone goes from A to B, gets there from here. I don't mean progress in the way some Christians adopt Plato's idea of spiritual growth, ascending from one level to the next, the soul as chariot soaring to divine heights. They baptize Greek thought in religious waters and measure growth upwards. The real path is more horizontal than vertical, a staggering back and forth, a drunk-stumble home.

We decided to tell Jonathan's story when we realized not telling it had plunged him into severe depression, had made him lose his faith. Had led him to believe it was okay with us to act as if nothing had happened. He had made the pastor a promise, but the pastor had broken his first. That wasn't what gave us the freedom to tell Jonathan's story. It was the fact that the church never had the authority to demand his silence to begin with. He was no longer serving there, no longer a member of the church. He had never intended to go to West Africa as their missionary; they jumped onto the last car just as his train was exiting the station. The associate pastor told us that because Jonathan was over eighteen, we had no legal authority over him. The only authority in his life now was of a spiritual nature, and they were its sole custodians.

The church felt we were too emotional; we couldn't think through things logically. Jonathan was told his viewpoint was subjective, having been the one who lived through it, but the senior pastor's perspective was objective, since he had done research on missions. "I concede that your son has suffered severe psychological distress," he told us from across the table, and then added, "I just don't think the conditions warranted it." And with that he was free, had washed his hands of it. It's the kind of upside logic that leads to abuse and only works when all parties buy into it. And we did. For a time.

When you are led to believe that you can't trust your heart or your instincts or even your experiences, then you become dependent on someone else's direction. In most cases that someone is a spiritual leader or leaders who are—miraculously—unaffected by emotions, good or bad, and are able to think and feel clearly for you.

They will do their best to invalidate your story. If that doesn't work, they will tell you not to tell your story.

What broke Jonathan's spirit in Honduras was different from what broke his spirit in Africa. He was desperately needed in Honduras, but unable to do much. He wasn't needed in

Africa; there was a charitable organization on every corner of the town he lived in, the medical clinic he worked with shared a wall with a bigger, better hospital. He was told he'd have every opportunity that eluded him in Honduras, and a year of his life to accomplish it all. It was a hoax, an illusion, and it led to a different kind of despair.

"Africa was going to be the redeeming of my uselessness in Honduras—it was going to be bigger and better and longer," he told me during one of our writing sessions. "Maybe it would get me out of the funk Honduras put me in. After Honduras, I vowed, 'This will never happen again.'"

It was that vow and his own sense of inadequacy—not his privileged lifestyle—that made him susceptible to the message of the radical movement, with its challenge to young people to sacrifice all for the kingdom of God. It was his vow that drew him to pore over books and scratch quotes onto his closet walls.

Jonathan wanted to save the world, save the little Honduran girl, and the key was to become a "real Christian" who would heed the call to radical obedience. This is what God wants of you, he read over and over again. There is no way you can fail. If you go where God wants you to go, you will discover new life.

"I felt as if I had found the way to The Way," he remembers.

He followed the formula and checked the boxes, expecting the advertised results. He crossed an ocean in search of the "gospel success" he was guaranteed.

But it wasn't an advertisement. It was the current bestseller in trendy theology, and it wasn't required to include the standard fine print. What was missing were the words: results not typical.

Jonathan, like most of his peers, would never fall for a behavior checklist. The old rules were simple, universal: don't smoke, don't drink. For some the checklist included bonus items: don't go to the movies, don't play cards, don't dance. Whatever the criteria, the message was the same: be good.

"A few decades ago, an entire generation of Baby Boomers walked away from traditional churches to escape the legalistic moralism of 'being good,'" wrote Dr. Anthony Bradley, professor of theology and ethics at The King's College. "But what their Millennial children received in exchange . . . was shame-driven pressure to be awesome and extraordinary young adults expected to tangibly make a difference in the world immediately. But this cycle of reaction and counter-reaction, inaugurated by the Baby Boomers, does not seem to be producing faithful young adults. Instead, many are simply burning out."[1]

Dr. Bradley made this observation after a long conversation with a student who was struggling with what to do with his life given all the opportunities—and the needs—before him. When Dr. Bradley published an article about the pressures placed on his students and others, he was deluged with messages from young people and their parents about the fallout of the new radicalism. He was shocked; it went far beyond the compassion fatigue he anticipated. "My inbox has flooded over the past week," he told me. "It's unreal the number of stories of wounded souls seeking relief."

"I continue to be amazed," Dr. Bradley wrote in the same article, "by the number of youth and young adults who are stressed and burnt out from the regular shaming and feelings of inadequacy if they happen to not be doing something unique and special. Today's Millennial generation is being fed the message that if they don't do something extraordinary in this life they are wasting their gifts and potential." And disobeying God.

The message, then, has changed from *be* good to *do* good. It's no longer "don't drink, don't smoke"; now it's "feed the poor, save the world." But it's legalistic moralism nonetheless. Of course, it's much harder to spot legalism when it's disguised as compassion. But the fruit is the same. What Jonathan and I came to realize—through our long talks, through the reams of note-taking and hours of figuring out—is that when the motivation changes from internal to external, from love to guilt, from freedom to bondage, that is when the lives of young people like Jonathan are destroyed— because legalism can only end one way.

Dr. Bradley agrees, "I was shocked by how many young adults had walked away from their faith because they figured they could never be radical enough for Christ."[2]

It's as if the proponents of the radical movement have set out to accomplish what Jesus was unable to. Through their books and conferences and podcasts they are trying to coerce the rich young ruler into sacrifice, into giving up his privileged lifestyle. To forsake comfort and safety to become a true disciple, a real Christian. But Jesus didn't use guilt. He didn't coerce. He let the rich young ruler walk away.

Of course it's one thing to discover you've been holding a broken compass; it's another thing to find your way home. Now we at least knew something we didn't know before: the first blow to Jonathan's faith was struck after Honduras. Because it was then he was most vulnerable to taking matters into his own hands.

Jonathan once said the rich young ruler was the devil in the books he read. When he came home from Africa, he tried to find the devil in his own story. First and foremost he blamed himself. He had done what the rich young ruler was unwilling to; he hadn't missed the call. But he had failed the test, which was worse. There was no gospel success, no transformation, no saving the world. Worse than nothing, he came home with an entry in the negative column, having lost his own faith. "I went to Africa with an expiration date," he admitted, because legalism is by definition taking matters into your own hands. It's trying to achieve spiritual results with a prescribed set of actions, by being good or by doing good.

After blaming himself, Jonathan blamed Peter. Then the church that swore him to secrecy, that decided he had outlived his usefulness. Then he began to reexamine the authors and the books that prompted him to give away all his belongings and to shake off the fetters of a complacent life and to travel halfway around the world—where he would only surrender to a new kind of captivity.

Then he blamed God, who was so disappointed in Jonathan that he withdrew his presence—both his displays of power and his displays of vulnerability—most likely in disgust. At least that's how he felt. Of course some of the suspects in the lineup were culpable for what happened to Jonathan. There was wrongdoing. There was isolation and control, manipulation and spiritual abuse. There was misuse of funds. But all of them, Jonathan began to discover, were guilty of the same thing: taking matters into their own hands. They had all resorted to a shame-based way to control others—or in Jonathan's case, himself.

Jonathan had assimilated the principles of the radical movement in order to control himself, so that he could manufacture certain results. This led him to put himself in a situation where he was then controlled by others, who also wanted to manufacture certain results. The blame rested not on a who, but a what. "Maybe there are no devils in my story," Jonathan told me one afternoon, "only legalism's uncanny ability to regenerate itself. Whatever new form it takes, at its core it's just old-fashioned manipulation."

The radical call to *do good* is how legalism gets to young people who couldn't be tricked any other way. "It's the gateway to my generation," Jonathan said. "What we are talking about is an ancient evil, not a new fad with a shelf life of another couple of years. Legalism doesn't fade; it just reinvents itself. I only carried the ideals of the radical movement to their logical conclusion, followed legalism to its only end. And it always ends in some kind of ruin. It always ends in despair."

As tragic as Jonathan's circumstances were, we realize now that the specifics of his situation only hastened the inevitable. Radicalism is unsustainable because legalism is unsustainable. Jonathan's particular experiences only accelerated that process. Overseas workers will tell you that it's not uncommon to find mistreatment or mismanagement in relief organizations. During Jonathan's time in Cameroon, he met a group of seven French girls who arrived in West Africa only to discover that the director of their supporting organization had run off with all their money. The girls had to subsist on their spending money until it was time for them to return home. Whites in shining armor, as they're sometimes called, are often taken advantage of. Jonathan's good friend, a young woman inspired by his trip, went to East Africa to teach schoolchildren shortly after Jonathan arrived in West Africa. The organization took her funds, garnered by support letters to family and friends, but limited her teaching time to one hour each day. The eyes of the indigenous teachers were ever on her; you get the sense they were tapping their feet or eyeing their watches until her time was up, anxious to get on with the real education, make up the time lost by humoring the pretty young missionary. Once she got her share of photos with adorable African children and enough fodder for her blog posts, they sent her home, their coffers full. But Jonathan's despair lingered long after he was safely home because it was the legalism he encountered in Africa that ruined him; it made it impossible for him to hide any longer from his own rigidity, from the monster under his bed. The sober truth is that what happened to him could happen to any Christian kid from any church or organization because in the end it was his misguided ideals, and not the particulars of his situation, that let him down. And those ideals are lived out at home as well as overseas.

After Jonathan returned from Africa, we learned from campus minister and writer Tish Harrison Warren of a bright, passionate young man who had committed to teach in one of the poorest, most crime-ridden schools in his state. Bolstered by the same rhetoric Jonathan heard, given the same guarantee of "gospel success," he worked day after day in the inner city to save those children society had failed. He eventually suffered a nervous breakdown. He moved back home and worked as a waiter. He and his friend Tish, a young radical herself, wondered what went wrong:

> We had gone to a top college where people achieved big things. They wrote books and started non-profits. We were told again and again that we'd be world-changers. We were part of a young, Christian movement that encouraged us to live bold, meaningful lives of discipleship, which baptized this world-changing impetus as the way to really follow after Jesus. We were challenged to impact and serve the world in radical ways, but we never learned how to be an average person living an average life.[3]

Legalism doesn't allow for average because it's an unyielding, never-satisfied taskmaster. Because at its center it is control, not love. Because it's the enemy of grace.

If you are trying to get there from here, you have to figure out how you got here to begin with. You have to retrace your steps to see how you arrived at the exact place where things began to go wrong. It's not a literal place on a map, like a Tolupan village in Honduras. It's the state of confusion and helplessness that took hold after Honduras. It's scratching away at the dirt, digging deeper until the root is discovered, finding what was below the surface motivating every action that followed. That took time. That took resources. That took caring friends and family who prayed and reached out and without even realizing it gave much-needed direction, a nudge west or east, or whatever was needed at the moment. And most of all, it was a mother and son who spent day after day, month after month, fighting or crying or figuring out but always talking, always wanting to get to the bottom of things, always wanting to know the truth so that one day they could shout it, share it, caution with it, heal with it.

CHAPTER 16

A COUNTERFEIT OF GRACE

IF IT WAS LEGALISM THAT shut me out, it was grace that snuck me in.

Life after Africa was painful. More often than not I felt confused and lost. I was navigating unfamiliar territory with no compass to guide me, broken or otherwise. Gone were the false guarantees, the empty promises I carried around like talismans for protection. I was now living in the tension between faith and doubt. And I was okay with that.

Some trials propel us to cling to certainty, while others propel us to embrace uncertainty. Legalism had been my certainty, my coping mechanism in the face of a confusing world, a way for me to avoid asking myself difficult questions. Without it, I had to learn to embrace a world that was no longer set in stone. I had to learn how to ask questions again.

Jesus came into a system that was black and white and made it gray. His vagueness was disconcerting, his stories had to be interpreted, and the temptation ever since has been to pin him down, to quantify a mystery.

Before Africa, I only saw the world in black and white.

Like the Pharisees, I could only see redemption in terms of what I had to do to achieve it. And just like the Pharisees, this preoccupation resulted in me missing the entire point.

The human tendency to focus on works must have been frustrating to Jesus. Some of his harshest words were reserved for the law. Jesus never softened the law because the law cannot be tempered. It always accuses. When it comes to the law, nobody wins, and that is why Jesus's debates with the Pharisees never lasted long. Arguing the law only succeeds in accusing the accuser, and in trying to trap Jesus with their rules, the Pharisees only managed to trap themselves. So when Jesus was asked law questions, he gave law answers. It was almost as if he were saying, "If it's law you want, then it's law you'll get."

Just as Satan, in the wilderness, tried to bait Jesus with the temptation of works, in some ways we're all part of the same diabolical plot to get Jesus off topic. Christians are still looking to Jesus for a checklist, a shortcut to righteousness. We still turn his message of grace into a message of law. But the law always paints into a corner, and when it does, the only way out is grace.

Rather than standardize every person's calling, rather than offer them a one-size-fits-all, Jesus embraced their differences. His grace was personal—it took into account a person's history, their struggles. For a rich young ruler, the answer might be to sell everything and give to the poor. For a Pharisee under the cover of night, it might be to be born again. For a woman caught in adultery, it might be to go and sin no more. For a demon-possessed man who is healed, it might be to tell everyone. For two blind men who are healed, it might be to tell no one.

And that is what grace does—it allows for possibilities. "Every journey looks different," a missionary friend in Africa once told me, "but that's how we experience our spirituality—it's the only way we know how to." Without grace, this wouldn't be possible. But by affirming our journey, Jesus is giving us the grace, the freedom, to walk out our spirituality in our own way, in our own time.

I think Jesus knew that when it comes to salvation, instructions do us little good. Worse, they make us feel like God is grooming us for acceptance. So rather than give us one answer, Jesus gave us many answers. Not to show us that the list is long, but to show us that in the end, the list is inconsequential.

Is there really just one thing we must do to receive salvation? Are there many things we must do to receive it? The mystery of grace, of course, is that there is nothing we must do to receive it.

If grace is unconditional, our standing with God is no more affected by the good we do than it is by our wrongdoing. God sent the law so that we could define good and evil. But God sent Jesus so that good and evil no longer defined us. And if the burden to not be bad has been lifted, so has the burden to be good.

That is why the gospel is offensive. Grace deems everyone worthy in a world that says no one is good enough. Growing up, I was told grace couldn't be earned—but I still needed to pray for it. I was told that all have fallen short of the glory of

God—but I still needed to be Christlike. I was told nothing could separate me from the love of God—but I still needed to draw nearer to him. Grace was not a gift to be given; it was a debt to be repaid.

But it is a counterfeit of grace if what Jesus did on the cross hasn't changed what's expected of us. He was the sacrifice to end all sacrifices, and the result is a grace that doesn't need to be paid for any more than it needs to be paid back. Nothing up front, nothing in return. No strings attached.

God doesn't ask for compensation because there's nothing we can give God that profits him; there's nothing we can do to match his gift of grace. And that makes us uncomfortable. We know that nothing is free, that everything comes with a price. We're cynical about grace, because we're not used to getting something without giving something in return.

The belief that we have to do anything to receive grace is the very antithesis of grace, which is given in response to our transgressions, not as a reward for our righteousness. If we were any good at answering radical calls to obedience, there would be no need for Jesus. But that is why Jesus came to liberate us. He liberated us from the need to be radical.

There was a time when I, like the Pharisees, only saw what I wanted to see. I was looking for law, and law was all I found. But when I read the Gospels now, I can't shake the feeling that Jesus didn't come to show us what to do but rather to show us what *he* was going to do.

So the question I found myself asking after Africa was, When did my relationship with God—this connection I strived so hard to attain—become about what I do rather than what he has already done? All I wanted was to please God, but I couldn't understand how he could be pleased with me if I hadn't done anything to earn it. All I wanted was a relationship with God, but now I realize I was digging for something deeper than that. Relationships are tenuous; they can be lost. Worse, they have to be worked for—they require effort and maintenance. No, what I have with God, I think, is something more like what Jesus said on the cross: "It is finished" (John 19:30). An act of love that can't be changed, can't be added to, can't be lost.

CHAPTER 17

HOW MUCH MORE DO I HAVE TO DO?

Laughter is the closest thing to the grace of God.

—Karl Barth

LAST NIGHT I CRIED MYSELF to sleep, laughing. That's not the way it usually goes. That's not the way the last year has been. Jonathan had closed the restaurant where he works, arriving home when I was already in bed. He stood at the door of our darkened bedroom, arms outstretched against the frame. But this time there was no third and final question of God, no declaration of his awful silence, his all-consuming absence.

Jonathan had a spiritual insight to share, a preview of which he texted me during his work break. The words were powerful, the message near perfect even though he tapped it out before rushing back to work. I added his words to our notes. We talked through his ideas for a few minutes once he got home, then he began to preach in a dramatic, exaggerated voice and to jump around the hallway like a TV evangelist, and Jeff and Emily and I laughed till we cried. I don't remember what he was saying or who he was imitating or even what provoked the outburst, only that this was joy spilling into hilarity, and it had been missing from our home for a long time. Jonathan went into his room and his preaching continued, high pitched and affected, and I cried in the dark and fell asleep, laughing.

There's no way to pinpoint when things began to change, since there's no way to see inside a cocoon while the transformation is taking place. Maybe it was when Jonathan was able to say Jesus again when referring to the Son of God. I noticed it almost as soon as he arrived home from Africa. He couldn't say the word straight out; it had to be Jebus or JC or something less intimidating, or less hurtful, than the real name. He was creating his own distance from the God who had distanced himself, who had put so much space between them that Jonathan wasn't sure he had ever been there to begin with.

Maybe it was the afternoon two teenage girls in modest skirts came to the door. I guessed they were either Jehovah's Witnesses or Mormon missionaries, which is why I hid in the kitchen. "I got this," Jonathan said as soon as he realized they were proselytizing. I was right about their intentions, wrong about who sent them. They were neither Jehovah's Witnesses nor Mormon missionaries. They were Southern Baptists, out canvassing the neighborhood as part of a youth group exercise in saving souls.

"If you died tonight, are you certain you would go to heaven?" they asked him, right on script.

"No, I'm not certain," Jonathan answered honestly, "but I'm optimistic, if God's grace is unconditional."

The two young witnesses blinked in confusion. There was nothing in their notes about responding to someone who had been stripped of the desire to be certain of anything, who had been freed from the illusion that words or works could secure your ticket upward. "Um, maybe you should talk to our youth pastor," they finally offered.

Maybe it was when he realized he had made it through three-fourths of Robert Farrar Capon's massive trilogy on the parables when for months he had been unable to concentrate for more than a few minutes at a time. Or that he wanted to read about the parables at all.

Or it could have been the day he was sitting at his desk, a 70s-style behemoth of solid wood donated by a friend of mine who knew he had given away most of his bedroom furniture. He was writing a chapter for our book, listening to his record player. He put on Jon Foreman's haunting *The Cure for Pain*. He used to shut himself in his room and play his guitar as he listened to that sad anthem—about running away from pain—over and over again before Africa. But not since. Not until this day. Maybe it was a declaration. Or a surrender. No more running way from pain—from selfishness in America, from inadequacy in Honduras. From perceived failure, from real rejection. From a silenced story.

> *And heaven knows, heaven knows*
> *I tried to find a cure for the pain*
> *Oh my Lord, to suffer like You do*
> *It would be a lie to run away.*

He played the song through, then put the record away for good.

Or perhaps it happened the afternoon he was running

errands around town and a thought struck him and he stopped to type out these words on his phone:

What has brought healing this past year is finally finding a name for what I'd done, for what had been done to me, and for what I do now.

I texted back: And what are the names?

What I'd done is legalism, which is when you control yourself.

What was done to me is manipulation, which is when you control others.

What I do now is grace, which asks for no control.

And with a handful of words he told the whole of his story: This is what sent me to Africa, this is what happened while I was there and when I got home, and this is the only way for me to heal. Unearthing the legalism is what made him realize he was holding a broken compass. But grace is what brought him home.

I sometimes wonder what would have happened if Jonathan had succeeded. I don't mean if he had stayed in Africa and equaled the feats of his missionary heroes. But what if his time in Africa, and the year of stringent self-denial that preceded it, had ended less disastrously? What if he had been able to hold his breath a little longer, keep to impossible standards for another week or month or year? He would still be moving forward, following a broken compass, bolstered by the good, if not lasting, works of his pharisaical rigidity. Success may have proved worse than failure; it would have only delayed the inevitable, exacted more flesh in the end. "I can see how belief in God doesn't have to end in despair," he confessed one afternoon. "I can see how an overseas mission doesn't have to end in despair. But I can't see how legalism can end in any other way."

Jonathan had shipped his own guitar in the crate that crossed the ocean, the one his donors had unwittingly paid for. It was a Taylor guitar, purchased with money he saved up from his first job bagging groceries at sixteen years old. He was home from Africa a week before I realized I hadn't seen it or heard him play it. I looked in his room, his cloister closet, the empty clubhouse in the attic.

At first he only conceded that he had left it in Africa. That didn't make sense because by then he knew the fate of the dozens of guitars he had brought with him; they were either being hoarded or misused. Why leave behind his own guitar? But he hadn't left it with the mission organization. He had met a young father while in Cameroon, a traveling minstrel named Eta who played for crusades and church events and whatever else was needed. He and Jonathan bonded quickly, playing a guitar duet at one of the crusades. Jonathan was surprised by Eta's musical interests, atypical for the people he'd met in Africa, and together they talked about folk music and Johnny Cash and Bob Dylan. Not long after Jonathan got settled in his new home, Eta's young son died and Jonathan never found out how or why. Death is so commonplace in Africa, and with it, a truncated grieving time that can seem almost cruel. Eta was called on to play at a church event just a few days after his son's death, and he went, as expected. Everyone moves on. The church community often adds to the pressure, since extended grieving conflicts with the ideal of the victorious Christian life, ever triumphant over the cares of this world. And so Eta put on his public face and played upbeat music and quietly bore his sudden, devastating loss.

Eta sometimes borrowed Jonathan's guitar to practice. He told Jonathan that he had once owned a Taylor himself, but it got smashed or destroyed in some kind of accident. Just before Jonathan left Africa to come home, he went to visit Eta. He wanted Eta to have his Taylor. To play at his events. To learn folk music and Johnny Cash and Bob Dylan. But most of all Jonathan hoped that restoring something to Eta that had been taken away from him would bring him comfort.

That had been Jonathan's prayer in his first days in Africa: "That's the hope I have," he had written in an early blog post. "If all else fails, I prayed, just let those who mourn be comforted." It was the very thing God had spoken to him as he waited on a patch of grass for his wrecked truck to be towed after returning from Honduras. Jonathan added: "We won't be able to reach everyone who needs our help on this earth, but God gives us the promise that he is still going to comfort them, and he's going to use you and me. That's why he put us here. We're here to love." Perhaps that was God's purpose for Jonathan in Africa from the beginning. Not the big, bold, brave thing, not something new and radical, but the simple promise God had given him when he was seeking an answer to the suffering in the world: blessed are those who mourn, for they shall be comforted. No one was healed of disease that night he ventured into the village to pray, but with his tears he comforted two boys who had lost their father. He didn't get to teach many guitar lessons at the orphanage, but with his guitar he comforted a father who had lost his son. The only lasting fruit of his time there was the only thing God had asked of him, intended for him. He walked through the countryside and comforted a farmer who didn't think he was good enough to be a Christian. And that was true in myriad other encounters. Not as the showstopper strutting the stage like the TV evangelist they wanted him to be, but as the person who walks through the crowd speaking love.

God had shown up in Africa after all. To bring comfort. To express *ashia*. To say, We are together.

Jonathan was among the mourners even then, but he too was disconnected from his grief. He put on the same brave face Eta had put on, but he would soon learn there's no real healing in that. There's no comfort without pain, without the acknowledgment of pain. His detachment only delayed his grief for a time. When he prayed that the mourning would be comforted, he was praying for himself. And for his mother and his father and his sister and everyone who loved him and missed him and wanted him back even after he came home. With that prayer he was anticipating all that would be lost while in Africa. Since Africa. The cure for pain—for him, for Eta, for everyone—is not running away from pain.

Because if you are able to reject the trite and the platitudinous, if you can withstand demands to stifle your grief and go straight through the pain, there is a resurrected God on the other side, waiting to compare wounds.

God's simple solution to the suffering in the world was comfort. And it was the solution to Jonathan's suffering as well. A comfort that first exposed the error of his thinking, especially his thinking about God, and then gave him the antidote, the balm he needed to heal.

That balm made its way into Jonathan's heart silently, invisibly. Thoroughly.

It came at night when his defenses were down, when his brave face had been set aside. It seeped into the fibers of his cocoon, loosening them, softening them until he woke up, laughing.

Jonathan had once dreamed of a little African boy in a wooden chair, a boy who emerged when Jonathan approached him and his clay husk loosened and fell to the ground. But now he realized he had taken from the dream something that was never intended, viewed the night vision in a half-light only. He interpreted it as a call to go, not as an outpouring of consolation and love and understanding. He only saw a boy in need, not a God who was willing to give. "I was missing all the signs, or maybe I just ignored them," he said when we first began to write down his story. "I should have been receiving the affection that Christ wanted to give me instead of trying to save the world. But it's too late for that now; that Jesus is no longer around."

Jonathan would have another dream, another chance, nearly a year after he returned from Africa. The setting of this dream was home, not overseas, and in it were two young men, including Jonathan, and two young women. One of the men was a friend who had also been through difficult times, had been taken advantage of. He had learned his lesson and had become a master of self-preservation. "If I could toughen up the way he has," Jonathan thought, "then Africa would have been worth it. I would have learned my lesson, and no one would ever take advantage of me again."

In the dream one of the women, a mutual friend of the other three, comes to visit Jonathan. When she sees the state of his bedroom, things strewn about on the floor, she begins to complain. She looks about for a remedy, decides the malady is a spiritual one. She suggests they study the Bible together, convinced Jonathan's rehabilitation is necessary to clean up his mess. "She was only looking on the outside, at the wreckage," Jonathan said, "and judging. She looked at me and could only see damaged goods."

In the next scene he is sitting in the backseat of the car with another young woman, also a mutual friend. In fact, she and the other woman in the dream are part of a triangle of love interests for the young man who had learned to protect himself at all costs. But this young woman doesn't see the wreckage, she doesn't judge, she just reaches across the seat and takes Jonathan's hand. She trusts him; she knows he will care for her. She never says a word, but like the clay-cracked boy in the wooden chair, she communicates something important, something pressing. She wants Jonathan to know that the purpose of Africa was not to toughen him up, not to thicken his skin. It was just the opposite. The purpose of Africa was for his compassion to come through intact. She tells him he is still able to care, and in a way he wasn't able to before.

Jonathan's self-destructiveness wasn't able to jolt his compassion awake. But now, the young woman tells him, his compassion has survived after all. It hadn't been up to him. It wasn't his choice to become hard-hearted or remain vulnerable. He didn't get to choose what would make his experiences in Africa worth it.

"The real epiphany of the dream," he told me the next day, "is that what I thought would redeem my experiences in Africa was becoming a different person, someone like my friend who would never let anyone take advantage of him again. I saw compassion as my weakness, an illness. But the answer I never thought to look for was the one I received in the dream: what would redeem my experiences in Africa was for my compassion to have come through intact—in fact, changed. It wasn't as if I had two choices, and I chose one and my friend chose the other. The message of the dream was that it wasn't up to me. It wasn't a choice I made."

The thread that ran through the dream, he said, was

one of providence, of knowing what happened to him was deliberate and served a specific purpose. It wasn't just an unfortunate set of circumstances but had intention from the beginning. There was meaning in all of it. And it was for this reason: that his heart, love, compassion be tested and proved, refined in the fire, not burnt up and left in ashes. His friend had preserved himself but had lost his ability to care for others. When the young woman reached for Jonathan's hand, she was choosing his vulnerability over callousness. The reward was not getting the girl, but being able to love the person in front of him.

After a few days, Jonathan admitted that there was another message in the dream, one that was too tender for him to talk about at first. More than providence, the dream was about God's care for him, his affection for Jonathan. "It made me think, 'Whoa, God still cares about me. I haven't been giving him the time of day, yet all along he's been working.'" That God cares for him was the very message he had missed in the dream about the little African boy.

"It made me feel things I haven't felt in a long time," he said.

He thought it was his duty to strive, to prove himself, but "God wasn't waiting for me, for my lead. I hadn't been asking, praying. I wasn't trying to conjure this up. It just happened. God was doing things the whole time whether I was praying for it, or even begging for it. It made me think: he's been busy in my absence."

Jonathan had finally received a response to his plea, "How long do I grovel at his feet? He's not there." And the response was, "I am here, whether you are or not." It wasn't too late; that Jesus was still around, had always been around.

"Even while I was dreaming it, I knew it was true. I knew before I even woke up that it was the real thing. This is what defines me now. Not the mess, not the struggle. I came through the other side with my compassion intact.

"Not because I did something to deserve it. I realize now that my relationship with God has always been a little superstitious. I saw our relationship as one of cause and effect. I always thought he was waiting on me to do more." The dream had nullified the if-then clause, the condition-ality of his relationship with God. It did so by redelivering the message in full light: "It was as if God were saying, 'In spite of what you do or don't do, look at all I'm doing and have done.'"

The conditionality was replaced by a sense of provi-dence, of preservation, but most of all, presence. And with it a relief that allowed laughter, welcomed it, brought it back into a home. And the young man who had slept on the floor of his closet and shaved his head and emptied his pockets and crossed an ocean realized that God had always loved him, had always been working on his behalf.

"And I didn't have to lift a finger."

Maybe there is a way to pinpoint when things begin to change, when a corner is turned. Maybe it starts with a dream and ends with a dream. Maybe it begins with a back-seat encounter with the God of the universe as a young boy and ends with a backseat encounter with the God of the universe as a young man. Maybe it's when you realize absence and failure and disappointment are perceptions. And that legalism always ends in despair. And to discover grace, to have it delivered to you in a dream as to the prophets of old, is to crack and shake off the clay and know the real God. The one who turns your legs into noodles and your pain into joy and your rigidity into grace. Who is waiting to compare wounds, and who lets you keep yours as he kept his, as a reminder of pain before change, of death before resurrection, of life that must be broken down before it can be built into something new. Keep them so that you never forget that what happened to you really happened. And that it's time to tell your story.

In his twenty-one years Jonathan had asked three questions of God.

As a young boy, he had asked: is he real?

As a teenager, he had asked: does he see?

As a young man, he asked: How long do I grovel at his feet? He's not there.

His dream had only addressed the second half of that plea: He is here, whether you are or not. But what was the answer to the first half?

"What I really meant by that question," Jonathan confessed, "is, How much more do I have to do to earn God's love?"

"And the answer?"

"I know it now," Jonathan said. "The answer is nothing."

EPILOGUE: SAVING THE WORLD

WHEN I WAS BACK IN the States, when I was ready to revisit the reminders of Africa, I returned to the warehouse where my journey first began. I wasn't dropping off guitars or loading supplies into cargo containers this time, but I did have a care package for my host family and volunteer friends, and I was leaving it in the care of the warehouse operator until the next shipment was ready to be sent out. As I pulled my truck up to the loading bay, the garage door retracted with a grinding shudder and the operator emerged. "Well?" he asked, shaking my hand. "Was I right? Did it change your life?" I thought for a moment and told him, "It did change my life. It really did. But not in the way I thought." He laughed. "That's usually how it works, isn't it?"

It's been nearly two years since I stepped foot on the red clay soil of Africa, and people still ask me if it changed my life. They want to know if it changed my faith, if the experience made me lose part of my faith. And the answer is both yes and no.

When I came home, I had trouble separating the words of Jesus from the words of the manipulators and legalists who had hurt me. And sometimes I still have trouble with that.

"Listen, we know what you're going through," some church friends told me when I came home. They were a married couple who had left my church for similar reasons long before I had, and as missionary veterans, they had experienced their fair share of pain overseas. "Looking back," my friend said, "I'll just say this: What happened to you won't become any less wrong, but it will become less painful." I asked her if it changed their lives, if their experiences made them lose their faith. "At the end of the day," she said, weighing her words carefully, "it's not that we don't believe, of course. There are just certain things we believe less, and some things not at all."

What I found is that the more I was able to distance myself from the demands of my Christian influences, the better I was able to recognize that my issues with Jesus were not so much about Jesus himself as they were about the Jesus culture. What I know is that my struggle to find the truth, my frantic need to have all the right answers, is gone. As Jacob wrestled with the angel, some people like to wrestle with their faith, to grapple with their doubt. But I don't see God as a fight anymore. No fear, no trembling, just rest. Jesus said his yoke is easy and his burden is light. And so it is.

In telling my story, I'm not trying to dissuade anyone from sacrifice—whether at home or overseas. Sacrificing for another is a profound gift. But I am trying to dissuade anyone from feeling there is a specific level of sacrifice required to be a real Christian. Jesus doesn't hold out his arm and say, "You must be this tall to ride." Jesus takes the bar set by the Pharisees, the bar that says, "You must be this good to become one of us," and he breaks it over his knee.

There are some things only Jesus was meant to do, paths he was meant to walk alone. It was Jesus's burden to save the world, not ours. In the end, it was only Jesus who could choose the cross, but it was a choice he made willingly. Obligation is a powerful motivator, but it can only take us so far. Conviction is stronger than obligation, and it is the only thing that separates sacrifice from slavery. This is where grace sets us free. It is in our very ability to choose that we find the strength to do so. Grace gives us the freedom to do good.

As for me, I don't know what the future holds. Sometimes I dream that I'm back in Cameroon, that I'm walking the streets at night again. It's quiet and the roads are clear; everything is exactly how I left it. It's a familiar scene, but in the dream there is one major difference: I'm there because I want to be.

I couldn't orchestrate my healing after Africa in the same way I had orchestrated my steps to Africa. I'm not telling my story to offer a new formula, because following a prescribed journey is what got me into trouble in the first place. It wasn't until I stopped trying to script my own story that things out of my control began to come together. And because I had no part in my healing, I have no solution to give. Seeing grace in a new light and learning to love the person in front of me is not a universal answer. It is simply what helped me. So instead of a solution, I'll just end with a story.

I was in Colorado recently to attend the wedding of a friend of a friend. It was the day after the ceremony, and some of us decided to go barhopping in the downtown district of Denver. Our last stop was at a restaurant, and I sat next to two of the guys in our party and struck up a conversation. They were both youth leaders at the same church, and seeing as the three of us had similar backgrounds, the conversation inevitably turned to God and religion. One of the guys, the more outspoken of the two, asked me offhandedly, "You're a Christian, right?" Not wanting to be painted into a corner that made far too many assumptions, I told him I wasn't sure how to answer him, that many concepts such as grace resonated with me. As I began to explain much of what I wrote in the last chapter, his expression grew increasingly indignant, until he nearly shouted, "C'mon, dude! Man up and decide what you believe!"

Much to the annoyance of the rest of the table, this outburst sparked a heated debate that would last the rest of the evening. But after the many hours spent arguing, and after the many, many beers consumed by my challenger, until his eyes were unfocused and bloodshot, I realized I'd already had this conversation before with someone else. In an instant, I was back in my former pastor's office, sitting across from him as he chastised me for breaking my promise and leaving Africa. From barking at me to man up to belittling my perceptions, bucking at me, and springing up out of his chair, the youth leader in Colorado was emulating my pastor, word for word, action for action. Not one detail was missing or out of place, even down to the trite "but I still love you, man" at the end, accompanied by a too-tight hug and a slap on the shoulder. It was like he had been following a script.

Before, I had been woefully ill-equipped to deal with my pastor's rebuke in any other way than to internalize the shame being dealt. And now, history was repeating itself in Colorado, only this time was different. I had found my voice again.

"Are you a Christian or not?" the youth pastor asked again. "It's not that complicated."

I have no confusion about whether I believe and would have been willing to say that I did, but I wasn't willing to answer the question the way he was asking it, wielding it as a weapon. There was more to my faith now than black and white. I had made room for complicated; I had made room for questions.

"Real men don't have to ask questions," he scoffed. "Real men can read the Bible and know."

"But," I pointed out, "didn't Jesus say to enter the kingdom as children, children who do ask questions, who don't have it all figured out?"

"At first, sure," he said. "But you can't stay there. You can't have childlike faith if you want to be a man of God."

Fumbling for examples, he finally turned the question on me.

"Well, look, what about you? Hasn't your experience with God changed since you were a kid? What was your first experience with God like?"

I told him the story of that fateful day in the car with

my mother, when I asked how I could know if God was real. I told him how she didn't shoot down the question, how she didn't just point me to the Bible, how she told me to ask God for myself. And I told him how that simple question left me paralyzed, how all I could do in that moment was to cry and to laugh. The youth pastor snorted, confident that he had trapped me at last, confident that I was going to prove his point.

"And what is your experience with God like now?"

A hush fell over the table. I looked around at my friends, and as the youth pastor smirked in triumph, I uttered the first thing that came to my mind. And as soon as I said it, I knew it was true.

It's still a lot of crying.

And it's still a lot of laughing.

ACKNOWLEDGMENTS

Writing with my son
Is like old-time prospecting:
I sift, he finds gold.

I wrote this haiku because it perfectly illustrates the division of labor in our book-writing process. But there were many more people involved in the life of *Runaway Radical* than its two writers. The story begins with Jonathan's first bold steps to Africa and ends with his first timid steps back to God. Both ventures required caring friends and family who supported him and us. To them we owe our deepest gratitude.

From Amy:

To Bill and Mary Lynn Lindner, for many prayers and much wise counsel and for being willing to fly across the Atlantic if need be to stage a rescue in the middle of the night. And to Beverley Bouchard, for releasing the funds to do so.

To Dean and Becky Northcutt, for giving us so much of yourselves and helping us through the most difficult days.

To Roxanne Romani, for the constancy of a mother's heart.

From Jonathan:

To Cheyenne Self, for knowing when to encourage and when to call out. Thanks for putting up with my ridiculousness.

To Nathan Quinn, for having my back, both at home and abroad.

To Professor Voytek Dolinski, for showing me the difference between a good idea and an interesting one.

From us:

To Trixy Franke and Bill Colwell, for your tangible presence and intangible wisdom during the days of disconnection.

To Deanna Dambrose, who early on provided the resources that gave us a framework to understand what had happened and the encouragement to move forward, even in the dark.

To Stephanie Drury, for creating a community of healing that made us laugh and cry and cringe and gave us hope. And to David, for helping us see the nonsense.

To Tara and Travis Lontz, for understanding, because having someone identify with your pain—and in doing so, validate it—is the first step to healing.

To Matt Baugher, our expert sculptor and publisher, who saw right away that there was more to be said, saw that the image already set in the stone had not fully surfaced and so began to chisel away, removing the last obstacles to Jonathan's story being fully told. Thank you for both your intuition and your expertise.

To Sealy Yates, agent and friend, we thank you not only

for the professional oversight of this project, but for your emotional investment, which was paternal and rallying at the same time.

To Sandy Vander Zicht, for your careful nurturing early on in the writing process, for your fingerprints on every page.

To David Hayward, for your art and your words, which helped us to escape.

To Jeff and Emily, for your encouragement and patience when the house became crowded with two impassioned writers instead of one. We couldn't have done it without your support and love. Thank you for picking up the slack. And for ignoring the shouting in the next room.

And finally and most importantly, to all those who supported Jonathan's trip to Africa—financially, prayerfully, wholeheartedly. We long to believe that, in the end, nothing was wasted.

NOTES

CHAPTER 3: THEY STILL NEED LOVE

1. Georges Bernanos, *The Diary of a Country Priest* (New York: Carroll & Graf, 1983), 62.

2. Charles Hart and Richard Stilgoe (lyrics), Andrew Lloyd Webber (music), *The Phantom of the Opera* (London: Really Useful Group, 1986).

3. Ibid.

CHAPTER 8: THE AFRICAN WAY

1. Philip Jenkins, *The New Faces of Christianity: Believing the Bible in the Global South* (New York: Oxford University Press, 2008), 95.

2. Philip G. Zimbardo, *Quiet Rage: The Stanford Prison Study*, VHS, directed by Ken Musen (1989; New York: Insight Video, 1991), VHS.

3. Ibid.

CHAPTER 11: THE ONLY CERTAIN HAPPINESS

1. Leo Tolstoy, *Family Happiness and Other Stories* (Mineola, NY: Dover Publications, 2005), 12, 30.

CHAPTER 15: RESULTS NOT TYPICAL

1. Anthony Bradley, "The New Legalism: Missional, Radical, Narcissistic, and Shamed," Action Institute PowerBlog, May 1, 2013, http://blog.action.org/archives/53944-the-new-legalism-missional -radical-narcissistic-and-shamed.html.

2. Anthony Bradley's Facebook page, accessed May 4, 2014, https:// www.facebook.com/profile.php?id=12720920.

3. Tish Harrison Warren, "Courage in the Ordinary," Intervarsity.org, April 3, 2013, http://thewell.intervarsity.org/blog/courage-ordinary.